ENCHANTED BOY

Richie McMullen is a trained senior youth and community worker with over fifteen years post-qualification experience. He is also a qualified counsellor and is in training as a psychotherapist. In May 1985 he founded the London-based Streetwise Youth Project which was the first of its kind in the UK to address itself solely to meeting the needs of young people caught up in prostitution. In 1987 he co-founded *Survivors*, the first male rape support group in the United Kingdom. His study on the subject, *Male Rape: Breaking the Silence on the Last Taboo* was published by GMP in 1990. *Enchanted Youth*, the sequel to *Enchanted Boy* is also now available.

Enchanted Boy

RICHIE McMULLEN

Acknowledgement

I owe my thanks to Anthony Masters for giving me the confidence to continue writing.

First published in March 1989 by GMP Publishers Ltd,
P O Box 247, London N17 9QR.

Second Impression February 1991

British Library Cataloguing in Publication Data

McMullen, Richie J.
Enchanted boy
I. Great Britain. Male Homosexuality.
McMullen Richie J.
I Title
306.7'662'0924

ISBN 0-85449 098 1

Distributed in North America by
Alyson Publications Inc.,
40 Plympton St, Boston, MA 02118, USA

Distributed in Australia by Bulldog Books
P O Box 155, Broadway, NSW 2007, Australia

Printed in the EC on environmentally-friendly paper
by Nørhaven A/S, Viborg, Denmark

Introduction

I have written this book because I have a duty to do so. I have been silent long enough. Silence, you see, is expected from abuse victims. The aim of this book is to contribute to the growing knowledge of child abuse. It is an unashamedly subjective account of the ten years of my life starting at age five and ending at age fifteen. It tells of how my own experience of abuse led to me becoming a boy prostitute.

I offer no interpretations. Instead, I offer you the facts as subjectively experienced at the time. I leave it to you to explore any inherent psychopathology. Just as I leave it to you to explore the psychodynamics.

I ask only one thing from you: That is, to suspend any judgements which this book may evoke within you. Not least, because every person in this book is, to some extent, a victim. The only questions worth asking are Why? and How?

Dedication

This book is dedicated to every boy who has been or is currently involved in any form of prostitution.

Mother's Milk

I'd been in bed for about a week when I heard my mother explaining to her sister, my favorite aunt, that I was ill. I was scared. Not of my aunt but of her seeing me the way I was. Their voices came nearer as they climbed the bare stairs, and as they did I put my mother's instructions into play. I got down among the covers, hiding my face, and acted as though I was asleep. Closing my eyes tightly I even tried to convince myself that I was sleeping but my heartbeat thumped and echoed in my ears. It was like a drum uncontrollably beating out the truth. I pressed further into the pillow as the door opened and my mother's voice was saying, 'He's fast asleep... Let's leave him to rest.'

My aunt came over to the bed and I felt her kiss the exposed top of my head. It felt both good and bad at the same time. Good, because she was kind and loving and I so wanted to open my eyes and see her warm friendly face. Bad, because I was scared stiff that she'd see I was awake and begin to ask questions and things. I didn't know if I could remember the story or not and I didn't want to cause any trouble. I was more relieved than disappointed when they left.

When the door closed behind them I waited until I could hear them downstairs before throwing the covers off my body. I was wearing only a shirt which I lifted to look once again at myself. The bruises on and around my bottom and legs were definitely getting better and my face only felt a little numbed now. I'd soon be able to get up. I must learn to avoid the buckle of the belt next time. It wouldn't be all that easy but I could do it. I could do lots of things without getting caught, so I could avoid a buckle dead easy next time. It was my own fault anyway. If I'd stolen the milk off a doorstep as usual then I wouldn't have got the belt in the first place, would I?

Thinking about that damned milk only made me feel hungry but I'd just have to cope with that. Instead, I shifted from the wet part of the bed to a dry spot and felt how good it was. It would be even better when it got warm. Yes, I could always get out of a mess, and like the wet part of the bed it was my own fault that I'd got into this one.

I'd arrived home from school very hungry and as usual the house was as empty as everything in it. I went into the kitchen to see what I could find. If there was bread I could dip it into the fat in the frying pan and have a feast. But today my brother James had obviously beaten me to it. There wasn't even a breadcrumb. Looking around to see what else might be available I determined to get home before him the next day. The door leading to the walk-in pantry under the stairs was open and there I saw the prize. On the top shelf, all by itself, was a bottle of milk, about a quarter of it gone. I knew the risks involved so I looked to the other shelves, already knowing there was nothing on them. The more I looked around the more beautiful the milk seemed to be. The mark on the bottle, indicating the level of the milk inside, stopped my stretching hand inches away as I stood tiptoe on top of the stool. I must have stood rigidly like that for a long time, just looking at the bottle. Then, all at once, I worked it out. It was a perfect plan. All I had to do was take a short swig from the bottle and then top it up with water. No sooner had I hatched this mighty plan than I'd had the swig and was on the way to the tap in the back yard to top it up, also taking a long drink directly from the tap. Putting the bottle back I checked that it was as before and that the level of the liquid exactly matched the mark on the bottle. It did, and I was confident that my genius had served me well. It just never crossed my mind that the shelf would be marked too. But you could bet anything you like that I'd check and double-check next time around.

Just as I was at the point of talking this kid in the street into parting with one of his sweets I heard my mother calling my name. Her tone informed me that my genius had failed me yet again. I knew better than to delay for a single second and the kid kept his sweet. As I got closer to the front door the facial expression of my mother filled the street and I knew I'd been sussed.

'Get inside! Where's James?'

I ducked and dodged below and between her long arms and the door post. I had just a second to do so in the knowledge that she wouldn't lash out whilst on view to the street. She never once hit me in a public place. Instead, she would fix me with her penetrating eyes and punish me when we arrived back home. Never once did she forget to do so.

'I don't know. I think he's in Billy's.'

I headed for the safety of a corner in the living room. She marched through to the kitchen and called me to follow, which naturally I did.

'Well?'

I looked at her blankly as I tried to hug the step between the living room and the kitchen. Half hoping, half praying that it wasn't to do with the milk. I stepped back very slowly.

'Where do you think you're going? What have you got to say for yourself?'

I silently stepped forward that one tiny step. Silence was always the best policy at moments like these.

'Bloody thief!'

When she grabbed me she vomited out all her pain.

'Two fingers the same bloody length! Thief!'

She slapped my face, body and legs.

'Thief, you'll rot in hell! I'll teach you to steal your own mother's milk.'

She was losing control and the blows became harder.

Much harder than ever before. So hard in fact that I had to scream at the top of my voice to bring her to her senses.

'Wait until your father gets in. Just you wait.'

She meant it. I became really scared and began to quietly cry.

'Get this place cleaned up, now! Make sure it's spotless before your father gets in. Bloody thief.'

I heard her lock the kitchen door and looked around to see what she'd meant by 'this place'. I could only think that she must have meant the pile of dirty dishes in the sink so I fetched a pan of water from the yard and began on them. The water like the room itself was cold. After what seemed an age I finally heard my father's voice. Then my mother's. They began to shout at each other and as with all the times before I couldn't make sense of it. I did, however, know where it would all end. In tears. My tears or the tears of my brother, James. He was nearly two years older than me and I wished for all I was worth that I was his age and could be at Billy's house right now. My father demanded that my mother put the kettle on and make him a pot of tea.

'If you want watered-down milk in your tea that's fine with me. That little sod in the kitchen has been up to his usual bloody tricks. I've had enough of it.'

The kitchen door burst open and my father's hugeness dwarfed everything around him. His smells of building site and pub were all rolled into one. He wasted little time looking at the milk bottle and tasting the milk before coming at me with his belt. I didn't move an inch. He was always worse if I moved. I waited for the belt to land across my back, bottom and legs. His grip on my arm was like a vice and I wanted to tell him that it wasn't fair to grab me like that. Getting the belt was one thing, being gripped like that was another. I didn't say a word. I didn't cry. I just kind of moaned like an Indian in a cowboy film. When he stopped I dropped to the floor like a wet rag and couldn't get up. He was telling me to get up but I seemed to fall asleep and woke up some time later in bed.

My mother was washing my face with a cold towel, and telling me that I'd fallen over and I'd have to stay in bed for a while. She was being very gentle and telling me that if anyone came I should pretend to be asleep and that I was a good boy. She searched my face for agreement. I loved it when she loved me and I nodded my agreement. She told me over and over again what had happened and what I was to say. It was a good story. Much better than the one which had happened. I preferred her story and let it enter into my soul. I had fallen and now she was looking after me. She was being so loving and I wanted her love so much. Whatever she said, I nodded my willing five-year-old head.

A Good Man, My Father

How can I explain my father to you? I guess real and unreal would be the best way, if you know what I mean. It was as though there were more than one of him but we never knew which one was coming home that night. When he got home the smallest thing could change him into one of his other unreal selves. He seemed to be in control of what he did but sometimes – sometimes – he would lose control and go crazy. That's when he'd throw his meals into the back of the open fire, shout and hit James and me. Then he would go to the pub. When he arrived home he would sometimes bring small gifts of peanuts or barley-sugar sticks. It was at these times that I could both love and hate him as one emotion. It was never knowing how he'd be which was the biggest problem. It was the waiting to find out which caused so much pain.

He was capable of doing the most extraordinary things. This was the man who held a huge crowd outside the church with the power of his passionate oratory. This was the man easy to love. During the service the priest had urged the congregation to vote Conservative in the next local election. My father held that crowd for an hour or more and convinced them that they should vote Labour. Labour won.

The living room of our house was often used as a meeting room where people would come to seek my father's help. His great ability in letter writing was much in demand as was his knowledge of welfare rights. He was always available to those in need, always ready to help the underdog, always giving of himself. I was so proud to be his son at these times. He was a man of vast contradictions. He was an active member of the Anti-Partition of Ireland League and had addressed huge crowds from the back of a lorry in the heart of Dublin about a non-violent solution to the Irish question as being the only right and proper way forward. I have a photograph of him doing this and will treasure it always. He was self-taught and angry about social injustices. He wanted to be a doctor and became a bricklayer instead. There was a time when he was devoted to his Catholic faith and became a lecturer for the Catholic Truth Society. His ability to hold crowds with his quick wit and sincere passion gained much admiration from me. He was a good man. In his heart he must have been. He just wasn't able to translate that goodness into his family. Perhaps it was 'the drink', which he took to after he was thirty and which provided the escape he so obviously needed. I feel sorry for him and perhaps you should too. Judge him at your peril. Judge him and you will fail to understand anything of what I plan to tell you about him. To judge him is to judge a piece of history, a time gone by. If you can, instead, love him then there is hope for all our futures.

Pigeons Can Fly. Cats Can't

It was the day after another beating and I was hurting as never before. This wasn't the hurt of physical pain. It was more a pain in the very centre of my soul. It was the pain of shame and humiliation. It was the pain of violation. It was a day when I found it difficult to get into my inner world. It was like going to the park and finding the gates locked. I knew how beautiful the park was but I couldn't get in. It was a Saturday. Saturdays were always difficult because they followed Friday nights. Saturday was the day my mother would scrub the doorstep and the house. Saturday followed pay-night, shout-night, drunk-night, pain-night. I hated Friday nights and I hated God for letting them come every week without fail.

That Friday night had been much as usual. The clubmen had come and gone. Some of them with their hire purchase payments, some without. The only two to be paid with regularity were the coalman and the insurance man. The others were rotated. One week paid, the next missed. James or I were the ones who had to answer the door of a Friday night while my mother sat shamed in the dimly lit kitchen out of the way. We told the lies we had to. Never once did these clubmen hear the truth. That is, that there was simply no money to pay them. Never once would my parents own up to being poor. They were ashamed, deeply ashamed of their poverty. Poverty creates the best of liars. My father would say, 'Never let the right hand know what the left is doing.' By this he meant, whatever it is keep it a secret. Never let the neighbours know anything. He trusted no one. He'd created an inner world in which his family were forced to live. My inner world was a much more beautiful place. It had colour, enchantment and magic. His was dark and sad. He put great emphasis on his children 'holding their tongues'. So it was that whenever we received a visitor to our home James and I were the perfectly behaved children. We were seen and not heard. Visitors congratulated my parents for having raised such fine children. James and I simply knew the rules and we observed them purely out of fear.

The movements of my mother's body and the tone of her voice were always a good guide to the kind of night we had in store. Tonight she was stiff and sharp. It was going to be be a hell of night for us all. She had the clubmen's payment cards laid out on the table in front of her along with the contents of her purse. Her pained expression told me clearly that as usual things didn't balance out. Her eyes darted from the clock to the payment books, to the front door and back again. I came to hate the chimes of that clock more than any other sound in my short life. Her eyes fell on James and me before landing on the coal fire, where they stayed. It was impossible to know how to help her or how to please her and all such efforts ended in her telling me to shut up. My father could have helped her far more. He was a rock, solid and self-contained. He kept most of his money for the pub and cards. His self-containment was something he cultivated with relish. I had not the slightest idea what he thought or felt about anything. Not knowing who he was caused the greatest pain to me. Was it going to be one of those nights he'd arrive home happy, bringing small gifts of peanuts or barley-sugar? It was doubtful. They were rare nights indeed. Was it going to be a night of death? I feared this quite seriously for I believed that one night he'd kill us all. Waiting to find out caused us all to be stiff and tight. We waited and waited and more than once I thought about smashing up the clock in the hope of stopping time.

Have you ever noticed the way pigeons seem to wait until the very last second before taking off when a cat is about? They seem to know that once in the air they enter into a world a cat can never know. I was the pigeon and my father the cat. I would open the wings of my mind and lift off into beauty and enchanted magic. He couldn't follow. He had no wings. However, Friday nights seemed to have the power to rip my wings off and the cat somehow knew this and could wait until it was ready to pounce. Sometimes, it would just walk around me and torment me with its power. Other times it would raise one of its giant paws and gash my already weakened body. There were those times too when having raised the giant paw it would hold it there threateningly, then with sadistic pleasure not do anything. So far, I'd been lucky. It hadn't killed me. What else would it have to play with then? If I could stay alive long enough I could grow into a bigger man than him and stop him hurting us and himself. If not I would kill him. Such thoughts tormented me for they brought gloom into my inner world. Thoughts like this had no place in magic for they destroyed it; evil had no place in my inner world. So powerful was the need to protect my inner world that I was forced to tolerate my father in the outer, unreal world of my existence. My inner world was absolute reality and he was nothing more than a bad dream.

The waiting was over. His key turned in the lock and in a second there he was, huge and menacing. He was a creation of every element known to man – though mostly ice. I caught the smell of beer and my heart sank. I moved closer to James. The smell of beer always meant trouble. His enormous clumsy movements spoke of anger. I wondered what caused this. I mean, did the beer liberate the real man or was the real man lessened by the beer? You tell me. Was he evil? Was beer evil? I mean, if evil exists what does it live on? I became confused by my silent questions. An eight-year-old shouldn't have to puzzle them out. But I knew lots of questions in my head even though I didn't know the right words to ask them of anyone else. Few adults understood this. I hated being a child. The problem with grown-ups is that they don't know how to make friends. Whenever I had a fight with James or one of our gang we could make friends again very quickly afterwards. When my parents had a fight their hostility seemed to grow towards each other and the world. How stupid they were.

If I had a fight with a kid who'd been a friend and it was obvious to us that we'd become enemies we just stayed away from each other. Why didn't my father just stay away?

No sooner had my father taken his coat off than the fight began. My mother made constant reference to the kids not having enough. I began to feel like a tennis ball. My father told my mother that she should manage things better and if the kids didn't have things then it was her fault. I felt terribly responsible for their fight. Simply existing seemed to cause them pain and perhaps if I didn't exist they'd be alright. Death seemed like a good way out. As the fight intensified they seemed to lose sight of just how forcefully they were attacking each other. It would fall to James and me to rescue them from the mess they were creating before something even more terrible happened. Their attention must be taken away from each other and redirected, but how? As though we'd found the answer, but more out of sheer pain, both James and I began to cry. We had the support of doing it together. My father's anger would be split and perhaps, therefore, halved. It was clear that our crying was irritating both of them and my mother ordered us to bed. This seemed to me like one hell of a good idea. We headed for the stairs and I was trying my best to become invisible when the cat spotted me.

'Come here, now!'

'For God's sake Charlie let them go to bed.'

We stood perfectly still in the hope that this time she'd win.

'Do as you're bloody well told, now!'

As always, she lost. We stepped towards him and stopped just out of range of his huge hands. We kept very close together. My efforts to redirect their attention had worked all too well. Our crying now was out of fear of what was to come. At first he ridiculed our crying and sniped that we were behaving like babies and not his sons.

'Stop crying,' he commanded.

'For the love of God Charlie...'

But we knew this game. He would force us to stop crying by beating us. My mother continued to plead.

'How in the name of God do you expect them to stop crying when you're scaring the hell out of them?'

Reason and logic played no part in this game though, and he countered with the inevitable.

'Stop crying or I'll give you something to cry for.'

The calmness of his order scared me even more for I recognised the danger signs. If we didn't stop now he was likely to kill us both. We tried and tried and his head movements and ice-cold eye contact told us that it better be quick. James was trying the 'stop breathing' technique and had almost completely succeeded, but I could see what it was doing to him. It would mean a massive asthma attack during the night. When they came he couldn't get his breath and we'd spend hours at an open window. At such times it seemed to me that he had to fight to stay alive. I would hold him and tell him about how we'd go to Formby and get some frogs, or how great a fighter he was, or how he could beat anyone in the gang. I would tell him anything to help him. It wasn't that long since he'd had an attack and I knew he couldn't take another. I opened my lungs and cried even louder. My father's anger would now be directed towards me and James would be safe, for tonight. Besides, I could get into my inner world and I wasn't sure if James had one. I wasn't being a hero or anything like that. Not a bit of it. By protecting James I was also protecting myself in a strange kind of way. I needed James more than anything else in the world and he needed me just as much. There had been times when he'd thrown himself between my father's belt and my body in order to protect me when he could see that I couldn't take much more. It was mutual survival. He protected us both and now it was my turn to do the same thing. My increased crying had already allowed him to breathe and he was controlling himself much better. I prepared for the smack I knew would come.

My mother's hands cupped around her strained face showed that she too knew what was about to happen. The blow came and knocked the wind out of me. Had I been able to fight back effectively at that time I swear to God I would have killed him stone dead. I was lifted high in the air as he grabbed me and threw me across his knees. I began to fight back for all I was worth but he held me easily with one hand. My mother was screaming and so too was James. Between blows he ripped away my only armour, my clothes. I continued to fight back in the fear that this time if I didn't then I would surely be killed. Within minutes I was all but naked and my flesh was stinging. I felt completely humiliated by his ultimate sadistic skill at exposing my body like this in front of my own dear brother. The blows were as nothing in comparison. A deep sense of shame flooded through me and I stopped fighting back. If he was going to kill me then there was nothing I could do about it now. In fact I wished him on. I wanted to die. But he needed me alive. He jerked his knees upwards and away from him and sent me flying across the room. My mother was screaming something about my clothes and James's eyes met mine. He looked horrified, which only increased my own sense of horror.

'Now get to bed both of you and don't let me hear a word out of either of you.'

James did his comforting job well but I felt deeply ashamed and couldn't answer him. I felt cheap and dirty. James tried to get one of our games going but I fell asleep to the sound of his voice telling me about cowboys. I woke some time later to move to a dry part of the bed. We were sleeping so close together that it wasn't possible to know which of us had pissed the bed. Probably both.

Yes, like I was telling you, it was a Saturday morning and the street was packed with kids. We'd got through the Friday night and now it was Saturday. Last night was in the past. It was dead. But the feeling of humiliation was alive within me still. Surely, I thought, this man can't be my real father. My real father would come one day and take me to my proper home. He'd explain to me about how there'd been a terrible mix-up and take me to a fine big house like the ones in my inner world. But I knew I was just day-dreaming. He was my father and they must all be the same. I had the strongest urge to go somewhere, to leave forever. But I was glued to the doorstep and soon my mother would come out and tell me to move so she could scrub it. I sat and watched the other kids playing. I knew my place and this was it. Where could I go anyway? I hated it but I was stuck with it. I could at least avoid the other kids for a bit.

I headed for the back entry and the back door of Mrs Jones. She took in washing and boys could earn a few coppers helping her turn the dolly peg. The dolly peg was a three-legged stool on the end of a pole which had two hand-grips coming out of the top end of the pole. Turning it was hard work and I hoped that today I could turn the mangle for her instead. I was good at that and knew when to turn so that she could feed the wet clothes through safely and swiftly. I would look at her while she worked. Her kids were all grown up and her husband was dead. She had white hair swept back and held in place by a headscarf. She was as strong as any man. She would talk away while working, telling stories about the past which I relished. She never asked questions and her stories would pass the time in a way which told me that she had her place in the world. She was content to do other people's washing and take things to the pawn shop for them for a tiny fee. She struck me as being the wisest woman I'd ever met. I earned a few coppers from her and headed for the shops. As I passed the door of our house my mother came out and without looking at me asked me where James was. I didn't have to break my silence for as she spoke James appeared with his best friend Billy. Billy fascinated me. His face was so proud and beautiful. She called James over and and then sent him on a message. As she spoke James was looking at me and I was looking at Billy. James's eyes then caught mine and smiling he said to my mother, 'I'll do all the messages today.'

I smiled my thanks back and my mother told him, looking at me, that he was a good boy. So he was too. They were back in no time at all and had with them a bag of bruised apples, which the shopkeepers sold for next to nothing. He handed them to me and I took one. It was delicious. After taking the messages indoors James was suggesting how we should spend the day. He whispered that we could go to the derelict house on the next street. I couldn't bring myself to break my silence, which James understood and took off with his pal. As they joined up with the other kids from the gang they reminded me of pigeons taking off into that space cats can never know. I was happy for them. But today I was beyond kids' games. Today I felt ashamed and dirty. I wasn't a baby and it wasn't fair to expose my body like that. All pride had left me. It was my fault. I'd set it all up to get James off the hook. It was my own damned fault. I'd made him do it to me. I was to blame. The filth I felt was me. Must be me.

From a Ragman's Handcart to a Taxi

By the time I was eight years old I had become used to the beatings from my father. After that last beating I had, as I saw it, no choice – I had to go away. It was perfectly obvious that my real parents just weren't coming for me. There was no chance of that now. No new clothes. No hot food. It was a foolish dream. But what the hell, I didn't need them. There must be lots of places to go, lots of things to do. I could go off and find a wallet full of money and take it to the owner and he would welcome me into his big castle and I'd become a prince and my father would have to kneel before me and I'd keep him waiting and I'd spare his life and... My day-dreaming was broken by the sound of voices. The milkman was talking to my mother. His hand roughed up my hair but I didn't object. It felt kind of good so I smiled at him. He was the only person who ever did that and I always rewarded him with a smile. I would often wait for him at the corner of our street. When he came in sight I would run up to him and he'd lift me up high onto the seat overlooking the horse. I would then ride my covered wagon down the canyon. When we arrived outside our front door he'd let me climb down all by myself and he'd rough up my hair. He always looked so smart in his brown overall, and his leather money-bag made him look very important. He never rode the cart himself. He never had to, for the horse would start and stop all by itself. It was a fine grey horse with enormous hairy feet. It wasn't as big as the coalman's horse, nor as handsome, but it was friendly just like the milkman.

I looked up from my doorstep day-dreams at the horse and thought it right that I'd not had a ride today. I thought instead about how good it would be to ride him like a cowboy. Ride him right into the screen at the picture house and join the other cowboys forever. I'd ride alongside of Tom Mix and kill all the baddies. I wished I'd had a gun. With the gun cocked I'd walk straight up to my father and put the gun to my head and pull the trigger. Then he'd be sorry. He'd cry and everyone would tell him off. Then he'd really be sorry. The milkman was gone and my mother was saying, 'Go on, go and play, I'm going to scrub the step.'

Play? Did she really think I could play? And then, what was the point in scrubbing the step? It was clean enough already. She always scrubbed the step after one of those nights though, just as she would scrub the living room. No amount of scrubbing would clean the house or me for that matter. None.

As I walked aimlessly towards God knows where my attention was drawn to Dago's house. We all called him

Dago but his real name was Malcolm Davies. His family were the first family in our street to ever go away for a holiday. While they were away our gang all climbed over their back wall and painted their windows black. The memory of this and of Dago's efforts to get us to confess caused me to smile inwardly.

'You'll never guess what colour they used,' he tempted.

We mentioned every colour you can think of, except black of course, and he was going crazy. He knew we'd done it, and we knew he knew. It was a great game.

'Green?'

'Blue?'

'Yellow?'

'Red?'

'Yellow?'

'Green with blue stripes?'

'Yellow with red dots?' We revelled in the game.

No response from Dago. In the end he gave up and told us it was black and we said that black wasn't a colour and he'd tried to trick us. He was a right nutter because he believed us about black not being a colour. It was great fun but we wouldn't have done it had he not rubbed our noses in it by constantly going on about their holiday before they went off. He was alright really.

I forgot about Dago when I saw the racker pass the bottom of the street and instinctively legged after it. A racker was a steam-driven lorry which made a terrible racket as it snorted its way along on its solid rubber wheels. Rackers often carried unrefined sugar which we called toggi-sugar and these were fair game for any kid who could catch them and get hold of the stuff by running after the racker, climbing on the back and taking a knife to one of the sacks. It was glorious stuff, fit for kings. This time, though, the racker was too quick and too far off to hope to catch and my attention fell, instead, on the ragman coming around the corner of the street. His call of 'Ja ranks' (jars and rags) had a free musical tone which lifted me instantly. He did well in our area and his handcart was already piled high with rags. He knew how to operate too. He paid kids in comics and balloons for the rags they could fetch from their homes. There seemed no shortage of rags and kids would bring him armfuls at a time. Sometimes the comics were American, in colour, and were worth two English ones in a swap. I thought the kids who preferred the balloons must be retarded or something. I mean, those comics were currency. What the hell could you do with a balloon? He was a colourful man, the ragman, and wore a scarf around his neck the way gypsies do. I'd heard about gypsies stealing children and thought about how thrilling it would be to be stolen away by the ragman. He was always singing and made jokes with the women which I never could understand. But they must have understood them for they always laughed. He seemed too nice to steal children, let alone eat them as the story went. All the women seemed to like him so the story couldn't be true, could it? It must be one of those stupid adult stories designed to scare kids. But perhaps not. Despite the jokes the women kept their distance and even the other kids didn't stay around him that long. Could have been the smell of the rags, I guess. Could be they really believed that he'd eat them. Daft buggers.

I was looking at the pile of rags on the handcart and found them strangely appealing. I wanted to be with them. To be in with the dirt and smell of discarded unwanted filth. Trancelike, I was drawn towards the handcart. At first I just stood by it as the laughing ragman collected the rags and handed out balloons and comics. Then I found myself holding onto the shaft of the cart. Reaching out I pushed the rags in towards the centre. They felt good to touch, to be near. I would go with them wherever it was that they went. I belonged with them. When the ragman raised the shafts to move on I took my chance, darted under and stood directly in front of him. Taking the enormous shafts in my small hands I half turned and looked up to him and pleaded.

'Let me push?'

'You're far too small, me ould china.'

'I can do it. I can.'

'You reckon eh?'

'Look, I can lift it easy,' I lied.

He made no effort to push me away and even roughed up my hair a bit. He must be okay to do a thing like that, mustn't he? It was heavy, real heavy but using all my energy I lifted it and pushed. It barely moved. I pushed harder still and it slowly began to move forward. Once it got going it wasn't half as tough. I was going to be with those damned rags even if it killed me.

As we moved off the ragman began to sing:

'There was a boy,
a very strange enchanted boy.
They say he wandered very far,
very far over land and sea.
A little shy and sad of eye
but very wise was he.
And then one day,
a magic day he passed my way,
and while we spoke of many things,
fools and kings,
this he said to me,
"The greatest thing you'll ever learn
is just to love and be loved in return." '

This song was called 'Nature Boy'. It came from the film *The Boy with Green Hair* and was written by Eden Ahbez.

As the streets went by the ragman tried all he could to get rid of me. I hung on for dear life. Not daring to let go I lifted, I pushed, I centred the rags on the cart and tried not to get in the way as he made his deals with comics and balloons. His skill at getting rags was impressive but I thought it unfair the way he conned some kids with his talk and laughter. They got only one comic or balloon when the rags they'd brought him were worth much more. I said nothing though. Still more streets and still more laughing. I was tired out and apart from not knowing where I was I'd become quite bored with the man. His laughter wasn't real at all. It was just part of his job. Turning yet another corner he looked down at me and said, 'Tired?'

'I'm okay,' I lied.

However, when he handed me six pennies and told me to go home I didn't put up a fight.

'Now, you know the way back, don't you me ould china?'

I didn't but said, 'Of course I do.'

I was done for. Completely exhausted. I couldn't have pushed that stupid cart any further. He laughed and sang that song again as he went on his way. I tried to make my way home. Home? I belonged with the rags...but not today. Today I belonged to the streets which all looked the same to me. I was lost. I had no idea where I was and became both thrilled and scared. There's no need to worry, I told myself. All I have to do is keep my eyes open for that wallet full of money and when I found it, as obviously I would, I would take it to the castle and become a prince.

Look as I might I couldn't find the wallet anywhere and when I sat on a low garden wall in abject distress a woman stopped and asked me if anything was wrong. I was seriously tempted to tell her that of course something was wrong, I couldn't find the wallet. I shook my head and said nothing.

'You alright, chuck?' she probed gently.

'Yea, I'm okay. Why?' I defended.

'You're not from around here, are you chuck?'

'So?'

'You lost, are you?'

She was all nice and warm and I wanted her to hold me in her arms and tell me everything was going to be alright. I heard myself saying, 'Mind your own business, can't you!'

She wasn't shocked or anything. She just said, 'What's

up, chuck?'

I stood and looked at her for a fraction of a second, but as I felt tears in my eyes I took to my heels and legged it as fast as I could. What was it my parents were always telling me? 'Children should be seen and not heard,' and 'Hold your tongue!'

I knew my place. I ran and I ran. It was stupid looking for a stupid wallet and I was stupid for looking for it. Everyone had their place and my place was at home with my family, right? Family? What family? A father I was terrified of. A mother who seemed to give all her love to my one-year-old sister Kathleen. My fourteen-year-old cousin who'd come to live with us and always went too far in play fights. He always hurt. My family was James, the brother just twenty months older than me. I ran and I ran. I was tired and wanted to rest but if I stopped and sat down then stupid women came up and asked me stupid questions. That's when I saw it – the solution. There on the other side of the road was a picture house. It was perfect. I had money enough in my pocket and there it was. I could always lose myself in the pictures. Could always get into the film. Perfect.

I ran across the road but before I'd reached the other pavement my heart had sunk down to my shoes. The picture was an 'A' and that meant I couldn't get in without a stupid adult. What was so special about being an adult anyway? They were just bigger and older that's all. Some of them were just big kids. I kicked the wall. Trying to figure out what to do next I walked up and down for a bit avoiding the cracks in the pavement. Then I figured that if I could walk backwards without standing on a crack I might find that wallet. I stood on a crack. Having lost the game I was forced to lean against the wall, finding as I did so that if I wedged my back between the bricks and the advertisement I could get a good position. I lifted a leg up behind me and tucked it under my bum and let my body weight fall onto it. My shoulders sank and with my hands in my trouser pockets I let my head drop so that my chin was on my chest. It was a good position and I could quite easily have gone to sleep. However, the noise made by the people going into the picture house was such that I couldn't. Besides, I could feel their eyes on me and didn't want them asking stupid questions. I kept my eyes down and looked at the shoes as they too walked on the cracks. If I'd looked up and into their eyes I'd have seen what they could see and I didn't want to see myself the way I was. Dirty and lost. I stayed there for some time.

An old pair of boots stopped directly in front of me and I stared at then as I had at the rags.

'Want to go in?' a voice asked.

I raised my head slowly. Slowly up from the old boots, the old trousers, the old raincoat, the old shirt, the old tie, slowly up to the old face. As I nodded my eyes met his and I saw myself clearly.

'Any money?' Old Boots asked.

I pulled out my fistful of pennies and held them out in the palm of my hand. Our eyes met again and without saying a word I asked him to take me in to the films. Taking the money from my hand he said, 'Come on then.'

The film had started and we had to go to the very front row to get seats. I'd never sat in the front row before and had to put my head right the way back to see all of the screen. I couldn't make out what the film was about but it didn't matter. I was inside and sitting down. No one would ask stupid questions in here and besides I was with this man, wasn't I? I felt my eyes getting heavy and let them close. I woke to the feel of his hand on my leg. It was on my thigh, just below the edge of my short trousers. It was just resting there and the fingers were making these small circles on my leg. It was kind of pleasant but felt strangely wrong so I moved my leg away. He instantly took his hand away and I was slightly disappointed. It was like being told half a secret and I wanted to know the rest.

'Like an ice cream?'

He didn't have to ask twice. I nodded. I was both pleased and relieved when he left his seat. When he came back though I was just as equally pleased and relieved. My confusions excited me. He'd taken off his raincoat and as he sat down, handing me the ice cream, the raincoat fell across my knees. I wasn't sure if he'd placed it there on purpose but as he didn't take it away when he sat down I assumed he must have. It seemed like a kind thing to do. It warmed my legs and it reminded me of the rags. It felt good. He must have known it felt good. Must have known I liked the feel of the raincoat on my skin. Must have known that I liked dirty things. Must have known that I'd been humiliated the night before. He must have done for he relaxed back into his seat and so did I. Then, when his hand went onto my thigh again, I knew for sure. I didn't move. This was the second part of the secret. His fingers went up under the edges of my shorts and touched my jimmy. That's what my mother called it anyway. Even though I knew that it shouldn't, it felt strangely good to be touched there. I was the centre of this man's attention and I enjoyed the role enormously. It was a tender caring touch and was better than my father's belt any time. The end of the picture came and I felt disappointed. The lights came up and as they did so he removed his raincoat.

Outside, the daylight had almost gone and Old Boots was asking me where I lived. The thought of home and my father swept me back into reality like a cold wind sweeps a bus ticket through the air.

'You look tired out.'

How right he was. I was exhausted and wanted to sleep but what was I to do? I was lost and had no idea where my home was. I said nothing. I knew my place.

'You run away or something, eh?'

Though I hadn't 'run away' the words seemed to make sense of the situation. I nodded my head.

'Like to come home with me?'

Once again I nodded. Other parts of the secret? My heart

raced. What the hell. There'd be food and a bed for the night, right? He was a gentle man and there was no way he'd hit me with any belt. We arrived at his front door after a ten-minute walk in silence. As he put the key in the lock he whispered, 'Be quiet as we go in.'

What the hell did he think I was going to do? Jump up and down and sing a song or something? I just wanted to get some food and go to bed. Perhaps he would look after me now, the way a father should. We went down a dimly lit hallway and turned into what should have been the living room but there was a bed in it. The room was bursting with loads of beer bottles, even a beer barrel as well as stacks of old newspapers. He closed the door behind him and put the light on.

'Wow, it looks as if you've been having a party.'

'Yes, I suppose it does.' chuckled Old Shoes.

'Have you? Had a party?'

'Yes, in a way. I bet you'd like a drink wouldn't you? Tea?'

'Not half, and with loads of sugar.'

'Sit yourself down, I won't be long. Loads of sugar, right?'

'Loads.'

I looked around the room for a place to sit. There was one chair and a single bed. I sat on the bed. It had sheets on it so he couldn't be poor. The room wasn't at all clean but he'd had a party. He obviously hadn't had time to clean up after it, had he? It must have been a huge party to account for all the bottles and things. He returned and handed me the cup of tea. It was hot, sweet and very welcome. He moved his coat off the one chair and sat down opposite me. Pulling the chair closer as he did so I got to smell his breath. It was worse than my father's. It stank! His free hand went to my legs and I let him rub it the way he had in the picture house. We finished the tea and he asked me if I was tired. I told him that I was and would like to go to bed.

'You'd better get ready then.'

His hands went to my pants and he began to fumble clumsily with the buttons. Stupid adult. He didn't know how to undress me. I always took my shoes and socks off first, then my jumper and shirt and then my pants. He was starting at the pants and that wasn't right. I pushed his hands away as firmly as I could, intending to stand up and do things the right way around. Before I could get to my feet he was a nervous wreck.

'It's okay...don't make a noise...it's okay...I won't touch you...'

I was utterly confused. Here was a pathetic old man as jittery as a wimp. His eyes darted from me to the ceiling and back again with repetitive jerks, his hands attempting to speak the words he just said all over again. Why was he suddenly so afraid? I suspected it must be something to do with the secrets.

'What would happen if I screamed?'I teased as I too looked up to the ceiling.

'Look...er...it's okay... Here, look...I'll give you a couple of bob...okay?...okay?...let's call it quits, eh?... There, take it...'

He thrust some money into my hands. He was so pathetic and for the first time in my life I felt the thrill of having an adult in my power. He'd touched me, that was it, and was scared of being found out. I would never forget this lesson.

'Okay,' I said calmly.

I stood up, tucked the money into my trouser pocket and pulled my clothes straight. He turned my stomach. I allowed him to lead the way to the front door and I left him there, sweating. The fool. If he hadn't gone in for all that stupid talk... Well, anyway he did didn't he? He did and I was now walking a dark street with no place to go.

I found my way back to the picture house and stood under the main entrance to get out of the rain. It wasn't heavy but I had no coat on. Before an hour was up I was being walked to the police station by an enormous policeman. He lifted his coat over my head to protect me from the rain and I thought how decent that was of him.

At the police station they were kind to me but they wanted to know my name. 'Hold your tongue,' right? 'Never let the right hand know what the left is doing,' right? 'Children should be seen and not heard,' right? 'Keep your place,' right? If I tell them who I am then I'll have to be me and my father will come and collect me. He'll beat the hell out of me for running away. I said nothing. Not one single word. When a policemen asked me if I wanted a cup of tea I just nodded. I wasn't daft.

They sat me up on a table and gave me the biggest mug of tea that I'd ever seen. It was almost too big and too heavy to hold. Once again I was the centre of warm attention and I loved it. Policemen came and went, some saying stupid things like, 'Who's this then?' and 'What's your name then?' I knew what they were up to. They were just like Dago when he tried to get us to confess about painting his windows black. I wasn't going to fall for that. I kept my mouth firmly shut. The policeman who found me came up to me and said, 'You know little fella, if we don't find out who you are we'll have to put you in a home.'

I was delighted! He had obviously tried to scare me but his words were music to my ears. It was everything I could ever wish for. A new home. No more belt. Once again I had learnt an important lesson. That is, if you run away from home and keep your mouth shut when the police pick you up they find you a new home. Fantastic! I looked into the policeman's eyes and hoped that he could see why I didn't answer him. He tried again a number of times, then took me to a room which didn't have any windows and told me that I could get some sleep in the bed. He left the lights on and the door open. I didn't undress. I just lay on top of the bed with a blanket over me. I'd never felt better in my whole life. I was asleep within seconds.

'Richard...Richard...come on, shake a leg...come on your mom and dad are here.'

I opened my eyes and horror filled me. There he was, my father. My mother stood slightly behind him, her face full of pain. I couldn't believe it. They'd promised me a new home. How did they find me? Why did they come? Why didn't they go away? I looked from them to the policeman for help. He smiled triumphantly. I screamed a silent scream.

'Be a good lad for your mom and dad... Go on, off you go.'

We went home by taxi. The first time in my life I'd ever been in one. Neither of them spoke and neither did I. There was no belt when we got in and I was allowed to go to bed immediately. James's breathing was odd but as I cuddled into his warmth he relaxed. I dreamt of pigeons without wings and how the cat always played with its prey before killing it. I pissed the bed that night and James never said a word about it or my absence the next day. Nor did I.

The remarkable discovery that 'running away from home' could change the way in which my father acted towards me was a discovery which may very well have saved my life. Being picked up by the police brought a momentary halt to the insanity of being beaten. It threw a spotlight on the family in a manner which didn't require that I tell the police anything. Indeed, I felt no great urge to tell anyone anything about my father for to me he was what a father was. I could see, could feel the difference in him after I'd run away. He became less hostile towards me and if that's what it took for him to be that way, then so be it. If running away reduced the violence then it was perfectly clear that I would have to run away from time to time. It was the most creative thing to be done if I was to survive his insanity.

Running away became a regular activity which no one outside of myself could make any sense of. The beatings would then stop for a time and a kind of peace would be arrived at. I could walk within smacking distance of my father and not be smacked. I would experiment with this and even try sitting close to him but it made little difference. He didn't seem to notice. He was somewhere else – in the newspaper, in the radio or inside himself. Talking to him was a complete waste of time for he would merely grunt a grudging reply. Never once did he talk with me about anything. He would talk at me, even to me but never with me. His world seemed to me to be the saddest place in the world. How lost he seemed. To have walked, just once, with him through a park would have been the greatest gift he could have given me. But he never once took me out anywhere. I never knew him to enter a shop for that was for kids and women.

His pain must have been almost too much to cope with, so he shared with me the only thing he had to offer, anger and violence. Never once did I see him happy or laughing. He spoke through his belt and I never understood a word. Running away brought him face to face with a reality he couldn't ignore. He could and did ignore me but he couldn't ignore the police when they knocked on the front door to inform him that they had found his son. It was a way of dragging him unwillingly out of his locked-up world, out into the reality most of us live in. I never knew his love and I grieve for it still. But as my mother would constantly remind me, 'Blood is thicker than water... We should all stick together.' That's fair enough I guess, but to ask a child to be a parent to his father is asking just too much.

Castles and Bandages

Running away had given me a brand new feeling. A feeling solely related to my father. It was the loss of fear. Somehow I'd come to know that despite his belt and the beatings he could never destroy my spirit. This spirit was the very centre of that inner world which often became my reality. In it I could do anything. Adults could be reduced to my size and I could always win. When this inner world was alive in me I could go off with the gang and really have fun. Fun which bound us together and kept adults away. The place which provided the most magic for me was an old derelict house on the corner of the next street. When we took it over it became an enchanted place. A place where a nine-year-old could become superman. My mother had warned me about going into the derelict because of the danger. What she and the other parents didn't realise was that it was the danger we were after. The danger mixed with our imaginations turned these places into adventure playgrounds. It was a place in which you could gain the respect of your friends by doing something brave. Like climbing the inner broken-down walls right up to the beams of the first floor and walking along one. Now that was brave and I'd never come across an adult who'd dare to do such a thing. My brother James did it though. Encouraged by us all, he did it.

I stood with other members of the gang and watched him. Holding my breath watching him, I lived every second and every move he took. I was terrified that he'd fall. The staircase had been burnt out by older boys and the beams which remained didn't seem that secure. The walls were loose and crumbly. The thought flashed through my mind that perhaps my mother had been right about this place. Only when James made it to the beams did I take a breath. A long intake of air filled my lungs with the taste of damp decay. The air in the derelict was like that and reminded me that each place has its own smells. In our church I could always smell incense even when they weren't burning any. When I let my breath go it came out like a deep sigh and with it went my mother's warnings. He'd made it. He was a hero and he was my brother. Not only had he climbed well but he had done so without any show of fear. I was so proud of him and knew that next time he had one of his breathing attacks in the night I'd be able to remind him just how brave he'd been in front of the whole gang. It would be the truth and let's face it he'd know it was the truth and that would help him, right? His attacks would mean hanging him half out of the open bedroom window where he would attempt to gulp air. He could never seem to get enough.

Now he stood there way above us, feet firmly planted, hands on hips and looked down with majestic pride at his men. He was today's leader, no question about it. We waited for him to speak.

'Come on, it's easy.'

We each looked at the other and knew that we'd have to climb. Billy Jones went first. Well he had to really, he was James's best friend. I hung back and felt fear rise up inside of me. Others followed Billy. Some made it look easier than others. It was the thrill on their faces which forced me to climb too. I wanted some of that. I too wanted to shout and boast and be king of the castle. I was the last one up and had climbed it much better than I thought I could. James gave me a knowing wink when I arrived at the top. He knew I'd been scared. Perhaps the others did too for they cheered. We were all together. All one. We were it. James and I could relive this adventure any time. Our heads contained an enormous amount of stories which we'd select out to tell each other in bed, when we were supposed to be asleep. We'd get under the covers and act out a story we'd created. Our sound effects of galloping horses were remarkably good, so horses often had to figure in the stories.

The derelict's windows were not bricked up on the level to which we'd climbed and the views commanded were, to us, magnificent. No one could take this place away from us. It was ours, we'd conquered it. We were proud and ready to defend it against anyone. 'Anyone' could have been Indians, cowboys, soldiers or anything. We were, in our own estimation, the bravest and the toughest gang around.

We were kings one and all. As we boasted and congratulated ourselves one of the gang spotted the possible enemy coming down the street. He called for silence and got it as we surveyed the enemy. Three boys. This could be it. This could be our first major war. Secretly, I hoped it wouldn't be because those three boys were miles bigger than us and could have had mates nearby. On the surface, of course, I was just as brave as any of the gang. Just as I was brave on the outside when a teacher broke up a fight I was in. Inside, I'd often be relieved at the intervention, but could never admit to being so. We ducked down so as not to be seen and following someone's lead we each began to collect bits of brick for ammunition. The enemy were getting nearer and would surely want to take over our fine castle. However they were not in the slightest bit interested and seemed to have other things on their minds. I, for one, was not that disappointed by this, but my relief lasted less than a second for one of the gang had known exactly what to do. He let fly with some ammo which landed directly in front of the enemy. The enemy knew exactly what to do also. They too armed themselves and the war was on. What a royal battle it became too. No one got seriously hurt in battles such as this but that seemed more by good luck than good management. After about ten minutes or so it was becoming obvious that we were running out of ammo. We'd pulled what we could from the loose brickwork and even caught the odd stone thrown by the enemy but we couldn't last out much longer. That's when the cavalry arrived. The pub opposite began to empty, the men coming out shouted at us to act our age and the enemy ran off. We'd won! We'd beaten bigger kids. Later we all but danced a celebration dance down our street. We were the best damn gang that ever was.

The sense of unity I felt with my fellow heroes, as we sat on our doorstep and relived the battle, was wonderful. Despite the fact that my bladder was demanding to be emptied I stayed with the gang until I got the chance to remind them that we'd nearly run out of ammo. The subsequent silence spoke of the possible consequences. Eric Connor suggested that we should prepare for future battles in advance. Colin Chambers said that we had to get the ammo up by the open windows. But how? It was difficult enough to climb without carrying ammo as well. After much searching the solution presented itself. The plan was simple. We had to get a rope and a bucket. One end of the rope would be thrown over a beam near the window and the bucket attached. The ammo would then be loaded into the bucket and hoisted up. All agreed that the plan was superb and the following day would see it put into effect.

The next morning our sense of unity was even stronger. The enthusiasm generated could have powered a speedboat. But where to get a rope? Ideas were offered and rejected as being either too risky or not risky enough. Billy Jones came up with the answer. The place which offered exactly the right degree of risk was none other than the haulage yard near the Commodore picture house on Stanley Road. We all knew our way around it having mucked out the stables many a time. The risk factor was just high enough to help us prove ourselves worthy of the challenge. We would employ the same technique we used when stealing from the docks, for there were many men employed in the haulage yard. The attention of these men had to be gained by half of the gang allowing themselves to be seen and nearly caught in the act of stealing something or another. The men would chase them and that's when the main raiding party would move in for the rope. Timing, we decided, was the important factor. Anyway, that's what we did and as on the docks when stealing fruit, the plan worked perfectly. We got our rope. It was enormous. Very heavy and very long. As we carried and dragged it through the familiar streets it was all for one and one for all. David Connor, Eric's brother, said we were the gang that could walk on water, but Dago said that that had been done before and therefore wasn't up to the challenge of such a fine gang. We fell about the place laughing. Dago could be funny when he wanted.

At the derelict an old bucket was produced from God knows where. Someone's mother would be mad that day. The rope was put over the beam and the operation of loading the bucket with ammo began. Half the gang went up on the beams to stack the ammo whilst the other half did the loading and pulling. What a team. Pulling the rope became the most prized activity and very quickly we worked out a plan whereby we all got to have a go at it. Because the leadership of the gang was determined by who had the best ideas or who did the bravest things the plan was reworked a number of times. It soon became a competition to see who could haul up the heaviest load of ammo. This meant that we each had to pull heavier loads than we actually wanted or needed to. The last of the gang to have a go was Eric. Just as I'd hung back the day before so he hung back today. He wouldn't be judged for that. He would only be judged if he didn't have a go. If he tried and failed that would be fine but if he didn't even try then he would face ridicule. Eric was small for his age and this was to be quite a challenge. After much eye contact all around Eric faced up to the demand. He asked for the bucket to be loaded. There was much relief for he was a prized member of the gang and to have had to ridicule him might have meant losing him. I loaded the bucket and shouted for him to heave away. Colin, who'd made up this game, saw that the bucket wasn't as full as all the others and demanded for it to be filled up properly. This he did without saying a word. He just looked at everyone and at the bucket and back to Eric with a grin. He never liked Eric as much as I did anyway. Eric told me to put more ammo in. I complied. Taking a firm hold Eric began to pull and take small steps back. It was clearly hard going for him as his breathing and tight movements informed us. But he was doing it. Bit by tiny bit the bucket was being raised from the ground. After what seemed an age it was just three or four feet away from the beam. Then he fell. Tripped up or let go, and fell flat on his back, letting out a loud scream as he hit the bricks and other rubbish. He confessed many weeks later that the scream was to cover up for letting go of the rope. In the moment that he fell and screamed I was struck an almighty blow to side of my head. In watching Eric I'd taken my eyes from the bucket. The blow sent me instantly into a bleeding heap. The strange thing is that I didn't scream or cry out. It was all too quick for that and the shock didn't allow for screams. No one spoke. No one moved. They too had received a terrible shock and just didn't know how to react. They looked glassy-eyed in one direction – at me. They looked like statues. I broke the silence.

'I'll have to go...'

I was about to say 'home' but realised instantly that my father was in the house and there would be hell to pay. James rushed towards me and threw his arms around me as though to push away the great gash in my head. He guided me to the street and when we were out of earshot of the others he spoke very seriously.

'You can't go home like that... If me dad sees you like that...in that state...he'll batter us...you know what he's like...he'll batter us.'

'I know, but what can we do?' I pointed to the gash and the great flow of blood.

'You've got to go to hospital or something,' Eric said, as he came closer with the others.

'But I can't go home...my father...'

'He told us to stay away from the derelict,' James explained.

The others seemed to understand but nonetheless insisted that I go home without delay and get help as soon as I could. It was obvious to me that the first place they'd turn to was their home if they were injured. This was my first major clue that all dads weren't the same. How could I then explain things to them? I couldn't. James too remained shamefully silent. He was fumbling for a response in his shocked state. He seemed more shocked than I was. He told the others to go home. That he'd find a way of dealing with things. It was almost worth the pain to have him say that. I loved him so very much and I guess he knew it for he gave me one of his winks. He'd spoken his words to the gang in a manner which bound them through honour to do as he asked. They left, silently and sadly. The pain on James's face as he searched for an answer was almost too much for me to cope with. His helpless feeling made him angry.

'Look... You... stay here and I'll... go and see... and...'

I knew that he was going to face my father and I admired his courage.

'Yes...okay. Go on then... I'll wait... here...' I said, pointing to the alleyway.

'I'll bring something, I'll bring... I'll bring... something,' he yelled as he ran.

I made my way into a back entry, a jigger we called them, and waited. What could he bring except an angry father? I waited. I knew that James would attract my father's anger towards himself in order to protect me. I loved him greatly for it. I put my hand over the gash and pressed down the matted hair in an attempt to stop the flow of blood. I'd been there only a short time when I saw Colin's mother running towards me. He'd obviously told her. I was scared stiff of the outcome of all of this. This wasn't keeping things in the family.

'Oh my God, just look at you.'

She began to hold me and lift me into her.

'Come with me, you're alright now.'

She took off her headscarf and began wiping the blood from my face. Her gentle touch evoked emotions I'd previously had little room to express. She reminded me of my mother when she'd wiped my face with the wet towel after that milk episode. I wanted to cry. She half guided me, half pushed me towards the street in a purposeful stream of warm comforting words. Nonetheless, I held back, digging my heels in.

'Come on, we've got to get you to your mother.'

Tears filled up in my eyes and my chest ached with my efforts to control my crying.

'What is it? What... You need your mother.'

'He'll batter me,' I blurted.

'Who? Your dad? No, no he won't. Listen my lovely, you're hurt bad already. No one will hurt you any more. He won't even touch you... I promise.'

'He'll kill me!'

'Your dad?'

'He'll kill me.'

She looked at me directly in the eyes then took my hand quite firmly. I was ashamed of my crying. Making it quite clear that she wasn't going to take no for an aswer she marched me out of the jigger into the street. I earnestly struggled to get away from her. She held me fast. Then I saw her, my mother. She was running towards us for all she was worth. I'd never seen her run like that. Her giant strides spelt out 'I love, I'm coming.'

'Jesus, Mary and holy Saint Joseph. Oh Jesus Christ almighty.'

Before she got to me and before she could say another word Colin's mum said firmly, and as though to a child, 'Get him to Stanley Hospital straight away. He needs stitches. It's more blood than wound, so don't panic.'

My mother held me very tightly and began to fumble in her apron. Colin's mum shoved money into my mother's hand and told her to be quick and remain calm.

'God bless you...' my mother cried. 'I'll see you later.' Meaning I'll pay you back when I can.

My mother all but carried me to the main road and the bus stop. Colin's mum knew that if my mother had to look in her purse to see if she had the bus fare then she probably didn't. At the hospital I enjoyed the attention and fuss as my head was partly shaved and then stitched. We took a taxi home. This was the second time I'd gone home in a taxi. I was sent off to bed the moment we arrived back home and it was made clear to me that I wasn't to be allowed any food that day. Just as I was about to climb the stairs my father said, 'Who else was involved?'

Without turning to look at him I replied, 'No one. I just went in and some bricks fell.'

'Get to bed' was all he said.

He knew I wasn't telling the truth and probably also knew that he was wasting his time trying to find out. James had obviously been banished to the kitchen because the door was closed over. It was only ever closed when one of us was sent in to clean up as a punishment or when people came to the house. Later, as I lay in bed, I could hear my father telling James that he'd been warned about going anywhere near derelict houses. Wisely, James said nothing.

'We know all about it. Your brother has told us everything about it.'

He had used this ploy too many times before to catch us out and I hoped James would remember.

'Now, we know all about it. So, I'll ask you just once, what happened?'

James had obviously opted for silence as his reply for I couldn't hear a thing.

'Get to bed! Now!'

Being sent to bed was the most regular punishment after beatings we ever received. To this day I hate going to bed early. James climbed silently into bed and we just lay close to each other. It was enough. Some time later my mother came quietly into the room with some food and told us not to tell a soul. We knew who she meant. We ate our feast and slept warmly, well and dry.

A Choice of Gods

They should have told us things, my parents. They told us nothing. Nothing, that is, about different religions or faiths. Most, if not all, of the people who lived in our street were Protestants. Or, as my parents referred to them, 'Non-Catholics'.

I couldn't make head nor tail of it. I knew that Catholics were the good ones because it was drummed into me at home, at school and in church. Yet all the gang apart from James and me were Protestants and they were our mates. It was crazy. Christ, we almost lived in church and the priest was a regular visitor to our house. Not, as you might think, to help a bombed out family, but to collect money for the church. Who the hell was 'the church' anyway? I'll tell you. The church was a building called Saint Richard's which the men of the parish built themselves, in their spare time. Into which they sent their wives and children to pray for the energy to earn money to give to the church. It was a place where we were taught what to think, what to believe and what to do. It was a place where all the local Catholics behaved differently and where the dominant Irish culture was passed on to us first-born English kids. It was a place where James would faint with regularity at ten o'clock mass. I would help get him out and head for the park across the road, where he would always make a remarkable recovery. Church was a place, then, where my brother's breathing and my thinking processes would be stifled by overcrowding and dogma. I hated Sundays for it meant at least two visits to the church. After lunch – the only good thing about Sundays – we, that is James and me, would be sent to Benediction. The church would be less packed for this and I have to confess that I often thoroughly enjoyed the service, especially the singing. Singing in Latin had its own special magic which I imagined could make brothers and sisters of the whole world. Absolute unity was singing in Latin.

The usual Sunday routine, after lunch, was for all the kids to play in the street. After an hour or so mothers would appear at their doors, call their kids in and then send them off to church. For James and me it was Benediction but sadly for our mates it was Sunday School. Can you imagine having to go to school on a Sunday? I genuinely felt sorry for them and would often express this quite openly as we went our separate ways at the corner of the street. So concerned did I become about this regular separation from our friends that I voiced it to James as we headed for Benediction. I was delighted that he shared my concern and we decided that the thing to do the following Sunday was to invite them to our church. We might, we considered, even convert them. We convinced each other that our friends would need only a hint of an invitation to come to a proper church instead of having to go to school and they'd jump at the chance. Once there, they would discover that being a 'Non-Catholic' was a serious mistake. It wasn't their fault really. It was their parents who were obviously to blame.

The usual game of kick the can was in progress the following Sunday when my mother appeared at our front door.

'James. Richard. Church.'

Other mothers appeared and repeated the same thing but they said, 'Sunday School.'

Before long we were at the corner of the street ready to say our usual farewells. I looked at James hoping he would take the lead. Well, he was older than me. He did.

'Why don't you come to ours instead?'

They looked at us in what seemed utter amazement, then at each other in turn. No doubt their stunned silence represented their gratitude at this truly generous and remarkable offer.

'What happens?' said a curious voice.

James and I hesitated. What a pathetic question!

'What do you mean, what happens?' I asked seriously.

'You know, what do you do?'

James took charge. He painted for them what I considered to be a beautiful picture of Benediction. He described the Stations of the Cross with solemn reverence. This would clinch it I thought.

'We have tea and cakes and things...' said Billy.

'Yea,' said another.

'Tea? At church?' I mocked.

'And cakes!'

James became curious and I feared for his soul as he asked, 'What...do you...do?'

I said nothing, but was just as keen to hear the answer.

'You know. Sit around and talk about God and things, then have tea.'

'And cakes,' reminded Eric.

'And lemonade... sometimes,' said David.

They now had our full attention. Seeing this they kept up the talk of tea, cakes and lemonade.

'Why don't you come to ours?' suggested Billy.

His suggestion was followed by a chorus of approval. It was a great idea, they thought, and anyway we were all in the same gang.

'And we won't say nothing to no one,' said Colin.

It struck me that this needed checking out, just to see what it was like. The tea, cakes and lemonade, I convinced myself, were nothing more than curious features. I wasn't sure what was going on in James's mind and looked at him with silent questions. This indicated to the gang that if James agreed then I would go along with things. They switched their attention to him. His token fight was superb. He agreed but on the pretext that it seemed fair to check their church out before they all came to ours. They accepted. It was marvellous – once again we were a complete gang. As we made our way noisily to their church James whispered to me, 'Cakes?'

'And sometimes lemonade,' I replied.

We quickly agreed that neither of us would say a word

about this to our parents. They wouldn't understand our plan to convert the gang to the proper faith.

At their church it soon became apparent that these 'Non-Catholics' had not the slightest idea how to worship God. Their church, for a start, was nothing more than a church hall. There was no altar and people were moving about. There was no priest, no candles, no incense. I felt very sorry for them and began to feel terribly guilty for not having got the gang to go to a proper church. I almost choked on the tea and cakes afterwards. There was no lemonade. On the way back home we spoke of the differences between their church and ours. Then one boy said something magical, 'I wish there was no such thing as Proddies and Catlicks.'

This comment gained much approval and caused a moment's silence. We were still in that silence when we turned the corner of the street and saw my mother. She saw us and turned back into the house. We'd been sussed. You see, Benediction didn't usually end until after Sunday School and besides, we came home from a different direction. James took in a gasp of air which he then skilfully exhaled as a whistle. I whistled too. The gang knew we'd been sussed and joined in.

'Where, in the name of God, do you think you've been?' my mother demanded when we arrived home.

We were perfectly aware that she already knew the answer to the question and said nothing. What was there to say?

'Your mother asked you a question. Now answer it,' my father said between gritted teeth.

We said nothing.

'You've been to the Bankhall Mission haven't you?' said my mother with disbelief.

As we nodded my father began to raise himself up from his chair and remove his belt. In an attempt to put off the inevitable my mother slapped both our faces and told us to get to bed and 'stay away from those Non-Catholics in future'.

'Have you any bloody idea what you've done?' my father demanded to know. 'We'll be the laughing stock of the whole street.'

We froze to the spot and as always tried to become invisible. But experience informed us that we would simply have to take what would surely come. We knew too that we had committed the most serious of offences. There was no getting away from that. My mother's diversionary attempt to get us away from my father was a good attempt but I realised it was no more than that.

'Who's first?' my father wanted to know.

Neither James or I volunteered, which my father turned into a kind of sadistic game. He selected James and took his vengeful belt to my brother's helpless body. I felt each stroke as they landed upon him. Fortunately the punishment didn't last long and James was ordered to bed. He quickly went. I judged that this punishment was somehow justified and it wasn't that severe. I could handle it easy. I would make no effort to transcend the pain by escaping into my inner world. I would take the punishment for I'd surely earned it. I allowed myself to cry and that seemed to please him.

My mother kept us indoors for two weeks away from the bad influence of Non-Catholics. I was heartbroken. Keeping us away from the gang was the greatest punishment and we'd already been punished once. It wasn't fair but then adults are rarely fair to kids, are they? Keeping us away from our friends was torture as was keeping us within striking range of my father. He made the most of the opportunity presented to him.

Not only was my father skilful at making the most of opportunities, he also created them. The one and only time I was ever to be alone with him in my whole life was when I was ten years old. My mother had gone to visit her mother and had taken James with her so that he could run errands. I was left alone in the house and was scared stiff. I tried my becoming invisible trick but that seemed to act as a signal to my father.

'Make me some tea,' he ordered.

I knew it. I just knew it. Whatever I did I was bound to get wrong and he'd punish me. But I didn't get it wrong. I made him a cup of tea exactly the way he liked it and took it to him proudly.

'It's too full. Empty some of it out.'

I knew it. Damn it. I just knew it. When I returned he took the cup from me without saying a word. I was safe. He took a flask from his pocket and filled the cup up with whisky. I'd not seen him do this before and thought it quite disgusting. I'd seen the flask many times before though. He drank from it often and always in a manner which told me that I wasn't supposed to notice. I hated that flask and all that it meant.

'What are you looking at?'

I said nothing and headed for the kitchen to busy myself with cleaning. That would keep him off my back at least.

'Come here you cheeky little bugger.'

The same old thing. Beer – whisky – violence. I went to him and was dragged across his knee. What the hell, I could take it. He pulled my trousers down and smacked my bare backside. As he slapped he told me that I had to learn. Learn? What? The only thing I was learning was to hate him more than ever before. He slapped on and on and I heard my inner voice calling me inwards. Calling me to beauty and safety. I followed the voice and went with it. Suddenly I realised that the beating had stopped. I attempted to get up and was instantly slapped again. He kept me there a long time and each time I attempted to move he slapped me some more. It was weird. It had never been like this before. I began to feel quite sick. Then he said, 'Go and get the butter dish.'

I was as confused as anything and as I climbed off his knee I looked at him questioningly.

'You heard! Get me the butter dish.'

As I pulled up my trousers and they touched my

backside I discovered that my bottom was raw. I tried to pull my bottom away from the cloth.

'Take them off.'

'It's okay, I, er...'

'Take them off. Do you want another slap?'

I didn't much care about anything. It was five years since he'd humiliated me by ripping my clothes off and now he was humiliating me by making me be the one to take them off. I took them off, went to the kitchen and brought back the butter dish. What on earth he wanted with it I had no idea, but the sooner I brought it the sooner I could regain my trousers and my pride. He took the dish and ordered me across his knee. The twister might be going to hit me again but he sure as hell wasn't going to make me cry. Not ever again. My inner voice called me again and I tried for all I was worth to follow it but couldn't. Jesus Christ! He was rubbing the butter into my backside. What in the name of God was he doing? He spoke gently to me for the first time in his life. I became scared as hell.

'You have to learn to do as you're told when you're told. You're not a bad boy.'

I was near to screaming out my confusion. My hate and my need for his love were all mixed up. I liked and hated his new touch. His hands became those of a nurse – caring and loving. But why then did I feel so much hate? As suddenly as he'd begun this weird touching he stopped, telling me to get dressed and go out and play. I was gone like a bullet from a gun and as I went I decided that never again would I be alone with him. Never again. I couldn't figure out why he hadn't sent me to bed. He always sent me to bed after a beating. This time he'd told to go out and play. Weird.

As I made my way to nowhere I heard myself telling myself that these weren't my real parents. My real parents were looking for me at this very moment and would find me soon.

Chinese Magic

My father wore stiff starched collars to his shirts which he changed twice each day without ever once unfastening his necktie. He would loosen his tie and unfasten the front and rear collar studs then slip the whole thing over his head. Never once did I see him without a shirt. Even when washing and shaving he would keep his shirt on. Very strange. He would tuck a towel in around the top of his open shirt and then shave. Very strange indeed. Anyway, the reason I mention this is because with fastidious regularity his collars had to be taken to the Chinese laundry to be washed and starched, and this was one errand I came to welcome. So much so in fact that I'd remind my mother that they either needed taking or collecting. This impressed her greatly for it prevented violent scenes of meals, and plates, being thrown into the back of the coal fire by my angry father. Remembering the collars saved many a fight. My remembering, however, was not for my father's benefit, nor, I have to admit, for my poor mother's. I remembered because it brought magic into my life.

The first time I ever went to collect the collars I was taken aback. At first because the shop was like no other I'd ever been into. There was no counter. Instead, on entering the shop I stepped into a tiny room about five feet square. As I did so the bell which was attached to the door signalled my arrival. On one wall, directly facing the shop door, was another door. Into that was cut an eighteen-inch square hole, on the base of which a shelf had been fixed. I was fascinated not only by this but by the wonderful smells which filled the tiny room. Smells of clean clothes and cooking all rolled beautifully into one. Everything was painted brown, a colour I'd never liked before. But here, it was just right. No other colour would have so enhanced this magical place. I stepped up to the hatch in the door and looked through. The walls in the main part of what should have been the shop were covered with shelves. Between the shelves partitions had been fixed which gave the shelves the appearance of boxes. All the walls were covered in these boxes. In most of the boxes were brown paper parcels tied neatly with string. I deduced these to be the cleaned and starched laundry. On the end of each parcel was pinned a piece of paper on which was writen something or other in Chinese. All those tickets were in different colours and made a most beautiful pattern. In my hand was such a piece of paper and after I'd studied it for a long time I tried to match it to one of the boxes. Before I could manage this, however, I saw him. The Chinaman. He was the strangest looking man I'd ever seen. His face, his beard, his clothes... I'd seen nothing like it. He smiled a smile of welcome. His walk was slow, like a priest saying mass. He was confident and calm and I felt myself smiling back. I couldn't take my eyes from his. We just stood there and smiled. It took some time for me to realise that he was waiting for the ticket. I handed it to him. As he moved to the boxes my eyes were attracted to his shirt, or was it a coat. It was silk and had a high-buttoned neck. It was the most beautiful thing I'd ever seen. He seemed to have all the time in the world and seemed as old as the world. His face though wrinkled had eyes younger than mine. They danced. His hair was the blackest I'd ever seen and the shine of it reflected the magic of the place. Handing me back a small parcel he smiled again. I took it and without taking my eyes from his I handed him the money. He had to look away to get change from under the hatch but as he handed me the change his eyes danced another smile. He bowed his head ever so slightly, so I did the same. He turned and went through to the back of the shop. I left the shop and walked home in a daze.

I found it difficult to get through the next week for my mind was constantly turning itself to the old Chinaman. I was punished at school for not paying attention and got my fair share of the belt at home for similar crimes. I didn't mind this at all for Saturday was getting closer and closer and my father's collars would need collecting. I had the most wonderful secret and I wasn't even going to share it with James. Besides, he was growing up real fast, just as my cousin who lived with us had done. He'd joined the merchant navy almost two years ago after working in a pawnbrokers for a bit. I envied him going to sea and I missed him greatly, even though he always went too far in play fights. This secret would be mine. I'd found a magic place. It was the most exciting secret I'd ever known. This was a secret which was nothing like the secret I'd kept about 'Old Boots'. I felt I knew the old Chinaman and yet not a word had been exchanged. How could that be?

Not concerned to meet the milkman's horse the next Saturday I told my mother that my father's collars needed to be collected. I walked slowly to the shop enjoying each step. It was as before. Nothing had changed, not even the smiling. This time, though, I pointed to the box the parcel had been in the week before. The old man looked at it and then back to me. He shook his head very gently. He could obviously see that this meant a lot to me, and as he took the ticket from my hand he pointed to the writing on the ticket and then generally at the boxes. So, it was the writing which indicated which box. As I studied the ticket he opened the door with the hatch in it and indicated that I should find the parcel myself. Amazing. I was to be allowed into the room of boxes. Silently, and for quite some time, I studied the ticket and those on the parcels then I confidently pointed to a parcel. His face lit up. He nodded. I'd found it. I could read Chinese writing. My heart leapt with joy. The old man was delighted and allowed this little routine each and every Saturday. He would even let me put the money in the drawer and take whatever change was due. But this was quite difficult. Not because I couldn't count and things but because he trusted me and I didn't want to make a mistake just in case he thought I was trying to cheat him. To counter this fear I would take less than I felt the change to be and he would then correct me. Never a word was spoken.

As time went by I became very good at reading the tickets and getting the right change. I got so I could do it as quickly as he did. But he was never in any kind of rush doing anything so it wasn't that hard really. In fact, doing things quickly didn't seem to impress him in the least so I slowed down. He approved.

On entering the shop one Saturday I instantly felt something to be different. There were voices. Happy voices. Many voices. Chinese voices. The lyrical sounds matched the new addition to the shop – a Chinese lantern. He came through, as usual, and was followed by six or seven others. They seemed to be a family. He opened the hatch door and I silently went about my business. After I'd finished they all applauded. All, that is, except the old man. The others had watched me and were obviously impressed. The old man had somehow been with me as I did things, as if he was taking part too. He wasn't just an onlooker. Anyway, I enjoyed the applause. It felt good. I felt good. The others began to move into the back room and as they did they beckoned me to follow. I hesitated and looked to the old man. His open face reassured me. I followed them into the back room. In the centre of the room was a round table. I'd not seen a round table before. The table was full of food and they were having some kind of party. I ate my first ever Chinese food. To this day it remains my favourite. One of the old man's guests spoke to me in broken English. She wished me a happy new year. She must have been daft or something because new year had been about two months ago. I laughed and tried to explain that it wasn't new year. They laughed and said it was. It was a wonderful party. Throughout the events I rarely took my eyes from the old man. After what seemed the right amount of time I explained that I would have to leave. They wished me happy new year again, mostly in Chinese.

Every week after that I would eat a simple rice meal with the old man. Always in silence and always alone. It was sheer magic.

Saturdays being Saturdays meant that they followed Fridays and I've already told you what they were like. Anyway, after one of our simple meals and with the parcel beside me on the table I didn't take my usual leave. I didn't want to leave. It had only been a few days ago that I'd run away from home. As was always the case the police had picked me up. Instead of finding me new parents – because I never spoke a word to them – they handed me back to my parents in the middle of the night. They always found me. I sat there in silence with the old man. He made no effort to encourage me to leave. For the first time he spoke. His voice was strong yet gentle. He spoke in Chinese and I listened in English. When he finished I told him absolutely everything about my world. My story was punctuated with customers coming and going. After he'd served each customer he'd return to the back room and indicate that I should continue my story. I told him about the unreal world of my father and the beautiful real world which existed inside me. I told him about everything and anything. I talked and I talked. I talked as I'd never talked before. Eventually, I cried. Once again he spoke to me in Chinese and held me gently in his wisdom. Later, much relieved of a burden, I thanked him and left for home. When I arrived home my mother asked me what had taken so long and where had I been. I just said:

'I've been to China.'

She looked at me oddly, shook her head and went about her business.

Each week after that I'd tell the old Chinaman everything. He always listened. I decided that I would help him in any way I could by way of thanks. He taught me to starch collars, the details of which I won't trouble you with. I tried to teach him English but our efforts ended in laughter each time. I tried to teach him to do sums as well for it was clear that they obviously didn't do sums in China. You see, he used a counting frame with beads on. He would slide these beads backwards and forwards and somehow find an answer. The bead frame reminded me of a child's toy. The kind of thing they put in front of babies in a pram. Teaching him to do sums became my prime concern but I have to tell you that despite my efforts and his obvious wisdom he continued to use his bead frame. Nonetheless, he rewarded my efforts by allowing me to serve in the shop. Never once did I get the change wrong. If the old man was in the front shop he would talk to me in Chinese and I would answer him in English. Customers would ask me if I understood him and I would answer proudly and truthfully, 'Yes, yes of course I do.'

Not long after this, when I was eleven, we moved to a different district and I grieved for the old man. When I finally got around to going to see him he was gone. A new family had taken over. A noisy family too. When I asked where the old man was they couldn't understand me nor I them. I was horrified at my loss. Or hadn't it all been just another of my magic dreams? I left the shop. That night the police picked me up twenty miles away in Southport.

School For Scandal

Moving house also meant changing school. This excited me quite a lot, not least because I was getting away from the crap of one school. James went to another school too but his was the senior school which meant that he was moving further away from me. On the first day at our new schools he walked with me and left me outside the gate of mine. Anxiety pulsed through me as I braved my way in.

Looking at the other kids told me nothing about them. They were much as the kids had been in my previous school, except this school had a different name. This was Saint Winifred's Juniors, which I considered to be a soppy kind of name. My previous school had been Saint Alexander's. So, from Saint Alec's to Saint Winnie's – what a come down! Stepping into this new unknown brought with it new hazards and I was scared. I avoided all eye contact since I was quickly sussed out as being a 'new kid'. The yard was packed and I felt like I didn't belong. It wasn't long though before some kids began to talk with me. They were mainly little kids so I told them to piss off and concentrated on my body posture. It was vital to send out the right messages. Most of the little ones moved off but this one little kid hung around and was pushing his luck. I told him that if he didn't piss off I'd thump him one.

'I'll tell our Frannie on you,' he whined.

The name Frannie meant absolutely nothing to me but it obviously did to the onlooking kids. Their faces told me that Frannie must be the hard case of the school. Shit! I'd only been in the place five minutes. What the hell, I'd known that I'd be tested out. James and I had discussed it frequently beforehand.

'Who the fuck's Frannie?' I sneered.

Saying 'fuck' was crucial. I had to be as hard as anyone in the yard.

'He's my big brother,' said the stupid little kid.

'An' he's cock of the school,' said another.

Holy shit! I was in it. Brave it out, I told myself. I had nothing to lose. I could take a good hiding and not cry.

'Fuck off! Go on, fuck off, you smarmy little git.'

He went dashing off, no doubt looking for Frannie. I lost sight of him as he went. It was important that I didn't follow him with my eyes for the others would have sussed that I was scared stiff. I was, but there was no way I intended for them to see that. All the swearing was hard work but if I wanted to survive this place there was no choice. Then I saw the little kid. He was leading the way over to me. Behind him came four other kids all about my own age. I figured the big kid in front to be Frannie. He looked as though he could take care of himself, but then so could I. Here goes your first fight, I told myself, so fight to win. I put my back against the wall and waited. As they got closer I picked on the one I'd figured to be Frannie and stared at him right between his eyes. When they were about six feet away I spat on the floor directly in front of him. He lost eye contact for a fraction of a second and I knew I had the edge. If the others didn't join in I could take him. My heart was pounding, my breathing erratic.

'Who are you?' Frannie demanded to know.

'Who's asking?' I countered to the space between his eyes.

'I am,' he returned to the same space between mine.

'Who are you?' I challenged.

'He's Frannie!' said the little kid.

Frannie acknowledged his introduction with a shrug of his shoulders and a butting gesture of his head. He was confident enough but this was his turf. Using exactly the same gestures I said, 'I'm Richie!'

There was no avoiding it now. There had to be a fight. I'd called his bluff and he'd called mine. There was no other honorable way out. I prepared to get the first kick to his balls. I knew that if got me first I'd be the lowest of the low for the rest of my school career. I had the slight advantage of being unknown and my adrenalin level was high. The thought of backing down didn't enter into my head. I'd had fights with bigger kids than this and done okay for myself. I knew that I'd be fighting for a position in the school and I was ready to fight like a cat. I also had the advantage of being ready for this moment for weeks, ever since I'd known that I was changing schools. He'd only had seconds to prepare. I could take him, I knew it. I spat on the ground again and was just about to send in the first kick when one of Frannie's henchmen said:

'I'd watch it if I was you. Frannie's cock of the school.'

I looked to the face which spoke and said, 'Who the fuck

asked you?'

'He's with me,' said Frannie.

'Need more than one do you?' I mocked.

'No I fucking well don't! Get this straight, smart arse, I'm the fucking cock around here...'

Before he could go on, I said:

'For the time being pal. You've not fucking beaten me yet. So don't push your fucking luck unless you can back it up on your fucking own!'

Absolute silence. Everyone, me included, waited for the fight to start. He wasn't in a good position to get a clear kick of my balls, I'd made sure of that. But I could get a kick at his the moment he moved.

'What's your name?' asked the henchman.

'Richie McMullen. Why?'

This seemed to have quite an effect on them. It was as though they'd heard of me. I went through the shoulder shuffle again and spat on the floor again.

'Go and get Richie,' commanded Frannie, smiling.

So he did need more than one, the bastard. Eye contact was maintained but he was smiling a weird kind of smile. Was he backing down? The henchman brought the other kid over. Everyone was amused and waited for Frannie to speak.

'Richie McMullen meet Richie McMullen!'

Everyone was laughing in a kind of wonder. The tension disappeared instantly. There wasn't going to be a fight. Everyone was telling everyone else that the new kid had the same name as Richie McMullen. My namesake and I fumbled for words to talk with each other. He struck me as being a really nice guy. I discovered that his middle name was David and I told him that mine was John. This was how teachers came to identify us throughout our remaining school years. Frannie and I checked each other out whilst all this new found excitement was going on. Neither he nor I had lost any face so we let it go at that. I'm not sure who was the more relieved. I was to be in the same class as both

Frannie and my namesake. Both he and I became kind of celebrities. Not only for having the same names but for both having stood up to Frannie. It was weird and kind of magical. You know what I mean? My standing up to Frannie was enough of a warning to any other kid that I was no easy pushover in a fight. I'd survived the yard. Now, all I had to do was to survive the teachers.

The kids had warned me that the form teacher, Dickie Moss, was a bit of a bastard, so when I joined the class I attempted to get a seat in the back. The teacher spotted me though and made room for me to sit in the front row, directly in front of him. I hadn't tried to get a back seat to hide from him or anything like that. What I was trying to do was find a place where I could get a view of the class. I wanted to see how the kids reacted to the teacher. As it was I had to rely upon my ears and the atmosphere for clues. The teacher looked me over and I looked away. No point in pushing my luck, right? I could feel his eyes burning into me and I got the message when he placed his cane in front of him on his desk. I thought him kind of clever the way he got his message across. I'd have to watch myself with this guy. I'd heard in the yard that he was some kind of war hero. His wrist bone was huge and looked kind of weird the way it stuck out. I thought of how difficult it must be for him to get a sweater over it.

On the third morning we began the day as usual. First with prayers, then the register and then an hour of religious instruction. We recited standard answers to standard questions from the Catechism. You know the sort of thing, 'Who made you?' 'God made me.' 'Why did God make you?' 'God made to know him, love him...' Anyway I think you get the message. So repetitive was this routine that I could allow my mind to drift off some place whilst reciting the answers. Suddenly I was on the spot. He'd asked me a question and I hadn't caught what he'd said. He began to walk up and down between the rows of desks. The class remained deathly quiet.

'When you're ready McMullen. I'm in no hurry.'
I could feel him standing behind me. If I told him I hadn't heard the question he would know that I'd not been paying attention. Before long his bony wrist hit my neck very hard and my face hit the desk just as hard.
'Pay attention!'
What to do? What to say? All the other kids could see what happened and I had another four years of school to get through. I must do something. I was in pain and I'd just about had enough of grown-ups anyway.
'Who the hell do you think you're hitting?'
He wasted not a single second in his reply. He grabbed and hauled me out towards his desk. He was a strong son of a bitch too. Picking up his cane with his free hand he told me to put my hand out. I couldn't lose face in front of the class and I had to prove that I could take whatever this war hero could dish out. Besides, I was a bit of a war hero in my own right. I put my hand out and kept the thumb lower than the fingers. I looked at him directly in the eyes but his attention was on my hand. I counted six blows. Six stinging painful blows. I didn't even flinch. I'd beaten the sod at his own game just as I'd often done with my father. Nonetheless, I was pleased that break was still some way off. It would give me a chance to recover. He asked me another question. I knew the answer but refused to speak. He made some snide remark which some of the kids giggled like girls about and left it at that. For the rest of the lesson I allowed my mind to ask questions. Questions like, is it fair that such a big man should be allowed to beat an eleven-year-old boy with his hands or with a stick? The answer was simple, no! But what could an eleven-year-old kid do about it? Perhaps more than they bargained for.
At playtime Frannie and his gang congratulated me, which I was grateful for. I stayed around with them for only a short time before putting my plan into action. Making sure that no one saw me I headed back inside the building and into the classroom. I took the cane and with

all my strength I broke it into pieces. I cursed as I did it. To this day I consider that act to be the bravest thing I've ever done. I knew all too well, you see, what would happen when they found out. So incensed with rage was I that I went to each classroom in turn and did the same thing. I wiped my eyes of the sweat, or was it tears, and went back into the yard in just enough time to hear the whistle. As we lined up in our class rows in the yard a teacher went up to the headmaster and whispered something to him. I was the only kid in the school who could guess what it was about. That made me feel strong. Then the headmaster addressed us all:

'Go back to your classrooms. Sit quietly and wait.'

All the kids were glancing around them to see if anyone knew what was going on. In our classroom, we waited our turn in silence. Ten minutes later the headmaster, the deputy headmaster and our teacher came in.

'During playtime canes were broken in this and other classrooms and I want the person responsible to stand up.'

Don't ask me why. To this day I still don't know why but I stood up. There was a general gasp of amazement in the class and I was taken off by the headmaster to his room. I knew what was to happen. He was going to beat the living daylights out of me but I didn't give a damn. I followed him through the school into the administration section where his office was situated. In his room, on his desk, was the best sight I've ever seen in my life. There, in all their glory, were the broken and twisted canes.

'Did you do this?' he asked, pointing to his desk.

'Yes,' I said without saying 'sir'.

He looked at me with searching eyes as he sat down behind the canes. I nearly burst out laughing, or was it crying? His face formed question after question. He nodded to the deputy headmaster who left the room and closed the door.

'Why?'

I thought it the most stupid question a grown man could

ask a small boy. It didn't deserve an answer. I said nothing. That was the best answer I felt I could give. His face changed a thousand times as he searched mine.

'You went around each classroom and...did this?'

'Yes.'

He looked lost in thought.

'Were you caned this morning?'

'Yes.'

The fact that he couldn't see what was plainly obvious made me laugh secretly with contempt.

'A teacher must have control of his class and the cane is a symbol of his authority...'

Here we go. Here comes all the shit. I interrupted him in full flight: 'It's not fair. I mean, it's just not fair!'

'That's the way things are, McMullen, fair or not.'

'It's not fair, that's all.'

It amazed me that I could talk this way to such a powerful man. I was beginning to feel good.

'A teacher must have control, respect...'

'What, by hitting kids! Hitting kids with... Respect? Who can respect a man who hits kids? It's daft,' I countered with unashamed anger.

'Yes, McMullen, respect. That is the way things are and what you've done is no way to change things. Teachers must have respect.'

I was still angry.

'Respect? Ugh! You mean just because they're bigger they can hit us when they want. They can just hit us. I bet you don't hit them when they've done something wrong, right? Yea! No, I bet you don't. It's just kids. Right? It's always kids.'

My anger was allowing me to say things I didn't think I was capable of. I was furious. So much so that I lost control and began to cry. I repeated my claim that it was 'just kids' over and over again, because that's the way it was. As I began to calm down he told me to sit down. I became confused. Where was the beating? His voice was gently telling me to sit down. It was weird. I sat down and broke into deep sobs. I was furious with myself for letting this man see just how vulnerable I was. I cried for what seemed an age. When I stopped he asked me, 'Does your father hit you?'

I wanted to scream out loud – Of course he fucking well hits me! You all hit me.' This answer was bouncing around in my head but I said, 'Of course not. My father's not like you lot.'

'What, not even the odd slap on the legs?' he teased.

'No! My father has never laid a finger on me in my life... He's always taking us out and... buying us things and... He never hits us... Never! He's...'

I was cracking up. I dried up. The headmaster didn't ask any more questions and told me that he wasn't going to punish me and furthermore that the class teacher would be instructed not to hit me again. This man had seen right through my defences but had left them intact. I was grateful and nodded my thanks. He allowed me to sit in the office for quite some time and even gave me a glass of milk. I fell asleep in the chair and he woke me to tell me that I could go home.

'Tell your mother that I said it was okay for you to go home. If she's worried she can telephone me.'

I went instead to the park and fell fast asleep in the sun. I dreamt of my father. You know I was telling you about how I wanted to look brave in front of the class when I was caned? Well, that was true but I left something out. It's the bit about not being able to answer the teacher's question. Well, anyway I'd always been real scared of answering questions for fear of getting the answers wrong. I guess it was to do with my father. The way he'd ask questions there was always a trick in it, if you know what I mean. No matter what answer I gave him, he'd have me. I just couldn't win. Everything was a kind of test, a game he'd play with my mind and he really scared me when he did it. It would get so that I thought I'd lied because I gave the wrong answer.

Whatever it was it was the wrong answer and he'd end up belting me. Anyway, that's what I dreamt about in the park that day.

After less than a year at this new school we had to do an exam called the eleven-plus. One look at the paper and I wanted to die. These other kids must be as clever as anything. I looked at the paper and knew that whatever answer I put down would be wrong. I know it makes no damn sense now but I froze. I put my name and the date at the top of the paper and that was that. I froze. I simply couldn't commit myself to paper. They'd have me then, see? I looked at the questions and tried to figure out what the trick was. I couldn't. Not one of the other kids in the class passed the eleven-plus either. Each and every one of us were transferred to Saint Winifred's senior school.

At the senior school we were the little kids now and had to watch our step with all the bigger kids. It was a weird place. There was this teacher there who used to make us stand real close to him behind his desk while he marked our papers and things. His elbow used to rub in the middle of our pants just like the old guy in the picture house. Well, perhaps not in the same way. I mean the old guy had been more honest about it really. This teacher pretended that it was just an accident. Sometimes he would take a boy into the stock room for the whole lesson. I was as curious as anything about what went on but not one of the kids in the class ever spoke about it, I guess because we kind of knew. That teacher suddenly left. He just didn't show up one day and the caretaker came to clear things out of his desk.

Shortly after that a policeman came to talk to us about not taking sweets and money from strangers or getting in their cars with them. I have to confess to being somewhat intrigued by all of this. Nonetheless, I also felt really quite guilty too because he kind of implied that if these things happened to us it was our own fault for not doing the right thing. He told us that 'the family' was the one place of safety we had and we should tell our parents if anything was troubling us. He had to be joking. Why, I wondered, had no mysterious stranger offered me sweets or money from some luxury car? You could be sure of one thing, from now on I'd keep a lookout for this mysterious stranger.

The next week we had a similar talk but this time from a priest. He went on and on about the sins of the flesh and about how evil it all was. I got a hard-on. All his talk about sex and stuff, well what did he expect? I got the hard-on and it wouldn't go down. Shit! What if he asked me a question? I mean, you always had to stand when you answered a priest. I was one of those people he was talking about. A sinner. A dirty-minded sinner who would burn in hell for my sins of the flesh. It still wouldn't go down. I began to recite the Lord's Prayer. It was still up. I tried thinking of other things but my view was always blocked by this giant erect penis in my vision. I looked at the priest as he thumped the table and there it was, the penis, huge and erect. My thoughts went to the gym teacher who always checked to see that we weren't wearing any underpants. He would pull our shorts away from our bellies and look down. When he slapped us with his slipper he always stroked the creases out of our shorts first and he would wait at the bottom of the ropes while we climbed both up and down. He would let his hands slip under the shorts. I lost the hard-on. I earnestly prayed that I would stop having dirty thoughts and even went to confession on the way home and told the priest about them. He told me to say three 'Our Father's and three 'Hail Mary's and one 'Glory Be'. He also advised me to join the scouts.

Fallen Hero

I have to tell you this. Not because I want to but to leave it out would cause you not to fully understand all which is to follow from it. I told you ages ago about my cousin, remember? He'd joined the merchant navy after having worked in a pawnbroker's. Well anyway he'd just come home on leave. He was eighteen, suntanned and as big as a house. I was eleven, going on twelve and was delighted to see him. He didn't go in for play fighting any more and so there was no chance of him hurting me as he used to. Besides, he'd changed. He was more grown-up about things. His shoulders were broad and he had a slim waist. Christ, he looked so handsome with that suntan. He told us about the places he'd been and the sights he'd seen. It was like being there. I was spellbound by his stories. I tormented him with questions and unlike before he took time to answer as best he could. When he went to get washed and shaved to go out with some girl I went to the bathroom and watched him. He stripped to the waist and lathered up his face. What a sight! He was a hulk of everything I wanted to be when I grew up. He had tattoos on both his arms. As he shaved, his magnificent muscles moved with elegant ease across his wedged back. Here, at last, was a family hero I could look up to.

He went out that night with his girlfriend and James and I went to bed. We still shared our big double bed from the old house and tonight my hero was going to share it with us. James and I decided to sleep at opposite ends. Each of us then had a chance to be alongside our big cousin. I prayed he'd sleep at my end. We tried like anything to stay awake so that we could talk with him but sleep overtook us both. I dreamt of being on my cousin's ship. He was the captain and I was the deck boy. It was a fine and wonderful dream.

My dream was broken by my hero climbing into bed. He chose my end. I was too tired to talk and was on my way back to dreamland when he pulled me in towards him. It felt wonderful as he cuddled closer. James would be furious the next day. I was fast asleep when he undid my pyjama cord but was wide awake by the time my trousers were around my knees. I became completely paralysed. I didn't know what to do. He must be asleep and think he's with his girlfriend or something. I dismissed this as I dismissed all the other possible reasons for what was going on. He put his erect penis between my legs and began to move it in and out. I commanded my otherwise paralysed body to move and it obeyed me. He was spoiling everything. God, dear God, make him stop. He was ruining everything, everything. I moved even further from him and lay on my back to protect my vulnerable backside from his continued probing. He could stop now and I wouldn't say anything about it.

His big strong arm reached out in the dark, grabbed me and pulled me closer to him. I was facing him now and he had the smell of beer. It was just like my father. He put his hand on top of my head and he began to force my head down under the blankets. He was naked and my face touched his penis. I jerked my head away in horror. Still he pushed me down and inwards towards him. I couldn't believe what was happening. It was insane. It was crazy. Nor could I believe how easy it was to cry so violently without making a noise. I know it's ridiculous but I didn't want James to wake up. Just as crazy were my efforts to pretend to be asleep. I hoped my dead weight would put him off. It was fast becoming obvious why he was pushing me down and inwards. I closed my mouth tight but still he forced his penis to it. The moment it touched my lips I burst up and out of the bedclothes like a human volcano. My silent crying was causing me great breathing difficulties and I was increasingly afraid that James would wake. My burst of energy only served to make him grab hold of me even tighter. It was just like the play fights of years ago. He was going too far. He pushed his penis between my legs with a vengeance and lunged into me. I felt dirty and guilty. It must, somehow, be my fault.

Suddenly my legs and backside were covered in all this sticky stuff and he stopped. The moment he stopped I flew out of bed and into the bathroom. I saw this white stuff all over me and my pyjamas. I peeled them off quickly and threw them on the floor. Whilst I waited for the bath to fill I used toilet paper to wipe his filth off me. I was now crying quite loud, protected though by the noise of the running bath water. The water was almost too hot but I got in and scrubbed and scrubbed. Drying myself over an hour later I still felt dirty. Why me? What was it about me that made him do that? What was it about dirty things which people seemed able to see about me? I felt dirty. Disgustingly dirty. I must have done something stupid to make him do such a thing – and that white stuff? What the hell was that white stuff? I cringed as I thought about it. What was it that I did to make him do it? Was I crazy or something? Perhaps I was just evil. I tried to say a prayer but I felt hopeless and worthless. I sat wrapped in a towel on the toilet seat and tried to make sense of it. I failed.

I went back to bed. Where else could I go? I hid in a corner of the blankets. Two hours or so afterwards I heard James getting up. It was morning. Very quickly after that my fallen hero left the bed. I pretended to be asleep. When he'd left the room I pulled all the clothes around me and tucked them in. I tried to forget, but failed. I couldn't get into my inner world either. I failed at every damn thing I tried. I was a failure. I must have dozed off for I woke with a start. My mother was saying something about the day being wasted while I rotted away in bed.

'Come on lazy bones, the day's almost gone.'

I turned over.

'Come on! I mean it.'

Try as I might I couldn't wish her away. She took hold of the ends of the blankets and pulled them off me. Jesus, I had no clothes on! I pulled them back to cover my exposed body and screamed at her to leave me alone. Then she realised.

'Where's your pyjamas?'

I'd left them on the bathroom floor and she must have seen them or else someone had put them in the laundry basket. I despised her for not seeing the obvious.

'Why aren't you wearing any pyjamas?'

I filled my lungs with air and without trying to cover myself any more I threw the blankets at her and screamed at the top of my voice, 'Because I'm not. I'm just not. I'm bloody well not! Okay? Okay? Satisfied now?'

She dropped the blankets I'd flung at her as though she'd been burnt and quickly left the room. She knew. And I knew she'd protect her sister's son. When I finally went downstairs and entered the living room my father and mother were the only ones there. I was relieved by this. They acted as though it was just another day. So much so that I began to question the sanity of the whole thing. Was I crazy or were they? Perhaps we all were. My mother broke my thoughts.

'Sit yourself down and I'll cook you a nice big breakfast.'

She had never ever made such an offer in her whole life. Why now? I knew the answer. She intended to deal with the situation by denying it ever happened. I felt even more filthy. I grabbed my coat and headed for the front door.

'Richard, your breakfast. Where are you going? Your breakfast?'

I slammed the front door behind me and I ran and ran. Later that night I was picked up by the police twenty miles away. I was sleeping on a bench in some gardens and they took me back to their police station. I was treated well and they were very kind. I kept my mouth shut as usual but nearly spoke to the policeman who came up to me and said, 'Has someone been doing things to you?'

I looked into this man's wise eyes and told him the whole story. The only problem was I didn't say a word. I told him with my eyes. He knew. He went off and brought me a cup of tea. It's still my favourite drink to this day. As I sat there my thoughts drifted back to the first time I'd had tea in a police station. Silently, I mouthed those remembered words, 'You know little fella, if we don't find out who you are we'll have to put you in a home.'

Perhaps this time they wouldn't find out who I was and I would be given a new home. My thoughts were becoming crazy again and I thought I would crack up completely. I mean, I knew my parents were my real parents but I couldn't shake the idea that somehow I had other, better parents who were looking for me. It was daft having such thoughts and they got me nowhere. But damn it, they persisted. Once again, they found out who I was and I was taken home in a police car. My fallen hero had gone back to sea and I was pleased about that. I hated him so very much but I hated myself even more.

I gave up all attempts to gain affection from either my mother or my father after that episode and relied instead on my inner world of beauty. My father had stopped trying to hide his sherry and whisky bottles and was increasingly hiding in them instead. We had a lot in common after all. I hid inside my head and he hid in a bottle. What a crazy family.

My father's drinking was getting worse by the day. How he functioned at work was a mystery to me for he could drink so much. He rarely seemed to eat and constantly reminded my mother that his mother had been a wonderful cook. He still flung his meals into the back of the fire when he arrived home drunk. He would then sit in his chair by the fire and drink even more. It was whilst he was doing this one Sunday that I think I saw him for the first time. That is, I saw his pain. He talked with massive aggression about his job – he was foreman in a building firm. I grabbed the opportunity to listen. He cursed the owner of the firm for being a Tory money-grabber. I asked him a few questions but his answers were given as though to himself. He was broken and sad. The thing he hated more than anything else was having to work for and be obliged to a Tory. For the first time in my life I felt pity for him. Sat in the chair was the saddest and most lost person I'd ever seen. It was as though, when I looked into his eyes, I could see my own son crying to get out. Tears filled up in my eyes. The sixteen-stone giant was nothing more than a lost child crying for affection. For a moment I felt his pain merge with my own and I think, at that moment, that I loved him. I went over to his chair and sat on the arm close to him. I had to speak to him. I just had to.

'That stuff's going to kill you, you know.'

He adjusted his huge frame and looked at me, then put his arm around my waist.

'Yes... Yes you're probably right son...'

This was the first time he had ever called me his son.

'Then why don't you stop?' I implored him.

He laughed. I heard only crying.

'You've no idea son...no idea...'

'Tell me,' I pleaded.

'One day.'

'I wish you'd stop. I wish you didn't drink. It just makes you unhappy. You know?'

'I know.'

He very gently removed his arm from around my waist and gave me a tender push off his chair.

'Go on now. Go on.'

I stood in front of him afraid, somehow knowing that this moment could never and would never be repeated. His pain was enormously sad. Tears filled up in my eyes and I unashamedly let them fall.

'Please stop. While you can,' I begged.

'Go on now. Go on,' he said again.

I knew he was telling me that it was hopeless.

'You could you know. If you really wanted to. You could.'

'One day. Go on now. One day, you'll understand and...' He didn't finish.

I turned and from the corner of my eye I saw my mother, tea towel in hand. How long she'd been standing there I don't know. She too had sensed the moment and her eyes were full of tears also. With a movement of her head she told me to leave them alone. Praying that here was a chance for our family to break through I picked up my coat and left them with each other.

I found myself walking. Just walking and lost in thoughts of the possibilities of having a healed family. A family without booze and violence. If I ever loved my father it was this day. I prayed for him and for us all. I think this was my first real encounter with hope.

Born Again?

One of the places I liked to walk and play in was the local park. I came alive there. The space, shapes, colours and sounds were regular mood-lifters when I was down. It was a place I could go to either by myself or with friends. Today I went to be alone because I felt alone. I felt shrouded by isolation. The old gang were gone. The old Chinaman was gone. Gone too was the tiny old house and its comparative poverty. I guess I was grieving. I walked through the park and saw, through the filter of my inner world, everything as one would see a film. It felt a bit unreal. I felt unreal as well. It was as though I was invisible.

A couple of hours later I went into the boys' toilet and straight into a cubicle. It was much as one would have expected a boys' toilet in a park to be. It was dirty. There was no toilet seat. It was damp. The walls were covered in all kinds of writing, most of which was about sex. I sat reading the dirty jokes but couldn't understand most of them. Some of them were really very funny whilst others were just plain crude. Others were simply stupid. All of them held my attention though. Scribbled on the wall were stories about sex. Male sex. As I read them I became quite aroused. That's when I saw it. There sticking out of a small hole in the partition wall was a folded piece of paper. I was intrigued and just looked at it. Whoever was on the other end of it was pushing it in and out of the hole. I pushed it back. It came back again. Weird. I pushed it back again and back it came again. I pulled it. It came free in my hand and I saw writing on it. It was a note and it read, 'How much?' I was baffled. How much what? I was still trying to figure it out when another piece of paper appeared. I dropped the 'How much?' note and read this one. It said, 'How old are you?' I was as curious as anything and kind of excited by this new game. At least I wasn't lonely any more. Whoever it was, he had my full attention. I waited for the next note which duly appeared but this time wrapped around a pencil. As I took the note I tried to look through the hole but all I could see was an eye. The note asked the first question again. 'How much?' Did he mean money? I hoped so but wasn't sure so I wrote back, in my best handwriting, 'What do you want?' This time I looked through the hole after I pushed the paper back and saw the vague outline of a young man of about twenty or so. I saw too that he had an erection. Very soon the note came back, 'I'll give you a couple of quid to see your cock.' A couple of quid was more money than I'd ever seen and just to look at my cock? What the hell. The notes began to fly backwards and forwards.

'Okay,' I wrote back.

'Okay, stand up opposite the hole.'

I kind of lost my nerve and wrote back, 'The money first.'

Miraculously the money appeared through the hole. The moment I saw it I knew what I was going to do. Pulling my pants up with one hand I grabbed the money with the other and legged it out of the toilets as quick as I could. Equally miraculously he didn't follow me as I ran through the park and then through the streets. My heart was pounding in my chest and I thought about what would have happened if I'd stayed there. I shuddered and thought of what my hero had done to me. This time though I'd won. I had the money and I didn't have to do anything for it. I was thrilled at my achievement. It was the quickest, easiest and the most money I'd ever had. I was trembling with conquest. Come to think of it, I'd have let him see my cock for that amount of money. The truth was I'd have let him see everything! But I didn't have to did I? I mean, I'd made him pay, right? The intense feelings I now had were amazingly like having a hard-on. As I thought more about things so I got one. Later, at home, I hid the money in my hiding place but checked it was still there about every half hour. It was, and each time I saw it I became excited.

The following morning I bounced out of bed full of life, much to the annoyance of James, and took a long hot bath. I found myself washing around my middle quite a bit. The duality of the sexual content and the conquest of the money began to play in my mind. As it did so I began to play with myself. I was completely aroused when James started to bang on the bathroom door.

'Come on Rich, you've been in there for hours.'

Perhaps I had. I had no idea. Later he told me that he couldn't understand why I'd taken a bath in the morning. I blushed and suspected that he knew I'd been playing with myself. I was deeply embarrassed.

'I just felt like it. Anyway it's better to take a bath in the morning.'

He let it go at that and even changed the subject. I couldn't get into what he was talking about though and my thoughts went back constantly to the episode in the boys' toilet. It was still electrically exciting. As I neared school, however, and we passed the church I began to feel as guilty as hell. The feeling was powerful enough to make James seem cleaner that I was despite my earlier bath. On the way home from school I went to confession but when I got to the main bit I left it unsaid. I just felt too guilty and ashamed. The damn problem was that the experience had turned me on sexually. It still did. I left confession convinced that I would rot in hell.

In bed that night I couldn't get to sleep for thinking about sex. Not only did I have an erection but it was hurting and wouldn't go down. I'd tried masturbating in the bathroom but I couldn't come yet and so gave up in despair. I knew a lot about masturbation because the boys in school, including me, had made it the topic of the year. The key question was, 'Can you come yet?' I couldn't. It was infuriating not being able to come. I'd tried a number of times with a boy called Pip in school but we got nowhere. Apparently you got this thrill and then you knew you could come. God, how I wanted that thrill to arrive. I'd long since figured it out that 'come' was that white stuff my fallen hero had left on me. How I'd like to leave some on him in revenge. James turned over in his sleep and the thought crossed my mind that he must be able to come.

Not long after that James was given his own room and I found it really difficult to get to sleep in my new single bed. I missed him enormously but we had to act all grown-up about it. Besides, he was going out with girls now. Yeuk!

Pip began to hang around me quite a lot and I guess I hung around him. We talked endlessly about sex in general and masturbation in particular. We spent time together in the library looking up dirty words in the dictionary. We continued to practise our new sport together in the toilets at school. I began to loathe him and yet would look for him every day so that we could do it again. We both came for the first time during the same week. Our sessions then developed into competitions to see who could shoot the furthest. This was a variation of the earlier boys' game of who could piss highest but a lot more fun. The fun began to wear off after a couple of weeks and we began to avoid each other. When we passed in the corridors we would avoid each other's eyes. I was convinced that the other boys, in this all boys' school, could see my guilty secret. One day, on the way to school, I met Pip and we went behind some shops and had a wank. It was weird because we never spoke. We just did it. As I passed the church just by the school I felt dirty, guilty and deeply ashamed. I knew that what we'd done was a mortal sin. By the time I arrived at school I was as depressed as anything. At the school gate I stopped. I don't know why, I just stopped. Kids were pushing past me to get in, but I was frozen to the spot. Without thinking about it I turned around and started to walk away from the school. Alan May, a kid from the same class, asked me with some degree of excitement where I was going.

'Away,' was all I said.

'What? You sagging school, like?'

I half came out of my dazed state and looked at him. He was a boy I'd never taken much notice of in the past and I didn't care for him at all.

'Yes, I'm sagging school.'

'Where you goin' like?'

'Why?'

'Y'know. Where you goin' like?'

'Wherever I end up,' I said, resigned that it didn't matter a whole lot.

'Can I come like?'

'Suit yourself.'

His excited nature balanced out and contrasted my resignation.

'Where'll we go like?'

His constant use of the word 'like' was a pain and his use of 'we' was not something I wanted to encourage. I didn't answer him. I didn't have the heart to tell him to piss off and hoped he'd get tired of just walking and piss off all by himself. As we walked he chatted on in a friendly enough way and told me how much he hated school. Every other word he used was 'like'. By the time we got to the main junction, where Merton Road crosses Stanley Road, he must have said 'like' a thousand times. I told him to hang on a minute, which was another way of telling him to shut up. He got the message. We stood in silence at the junction while I allowed my thoughts to replay old games. This was one of those junctions I'd waited at many times in the past. It was a good place, you see, for skipping wagons. That is, jumpimg on the backs of wagons as they slowed or stopped at the traffic lights. We did this either just for the fun of it or for toggi-sugar. Anyway, there we were standing at the junction when the wagon stopped at the lights dragged me out of my thoughts. I reacted instinctively.

'Come on.'

I sprang onto the back of the now moving wagon which took Alan by complete surprise. He was legging after it and I was screaming encouragement. He made it and we both laughed with joy. That was it, you see, instant joy! Then we began to sing our heads off and jeered at the disapproving older pedestrians. All our problems were left at the junction for we were now in a world of our own, a new and exciting world. Despite this new-found joy I experienced a kind of calm which disturbed me but which I didn't allow to surface. It was as though every worry and problem I'd ever had was gone and I was heading for a new life. Our singing and laughter died after a while and we drifted into a long period of silence. Alan started to complain after about an hour or so. Mostly of the cold. He was becoming a pain again.

'Look if you don't like it get off at the next set of lights and piss off, okay!'

He shut up. I'd made up my mind that I was going to go wherever it was that the wagon was going. This was not going to be one of those times when the police picked me up twenty miles from home. We'd already gone at least fifty miles and I had a whole new life waiting for me. Alan was welcome to come along or get off. It was his choice and he'd made it. I suspect the only reason he stayed on was because he didn't want to lose face. He should have got off.

A couple of hours later the wagon pulled into a market in a place called Oldham. The driver switched off the engine which was our signal to get off and out of sight smartly. Alan was relieved and I was disappointed that we hadn't gone much further. We stole some food from the stalls and laughed at the accents of the people. Alan began to mimick the Oldham accent, which according to him was all

'Ee-bah-gum', and I fell about the place. He had remarkable talent but mistook my laughter for intimacy and began to speak to me as though I was his best friend. I had no best friend. He got the conversation around to going home and I called him chicken. He was deeply hurt and sulked for a long time. Long enough for me to regret having said it to him and for me to suggest that perhaps it might be a good idea to skip a wagon back home. This lifted him and he told me that we could always do it again some time. Yes, that's true, I thought, but not with you. We looked around the market for a wagon which had a Liverpool address and found one. We waited until it started to move out of the market and jumped on the back. After about ten minutes or so Alan began to panic.

'It's goin' the wrong bloody way!'

'It doesn't matter,' I called out to reassure him.

'But we could end up anywhere like.'

'It doesn't matter.'

But it obviously did to Alan who kept on and on about it.

'It could be goin' anywhere,' he insisted.

The thought warmed me. Anywhere was a better place to be.

'Richie, let's get off this one and get another. Okay, Richie?'

It didn't make much difference to me so I agreed and he stopped panicking and thanked me. We agreed to get off at the next set of lights. That calmed him down. Fifteen minutes later the wagon hadn't stopped. It was fairly flying through green light after green light. Alan began to panic again.

'What're we gunna do now like?' he demanded to know.

'Look when it slows down next time we'll jump it, okay,' I called. Anything to shut him up.

The wagon slowed and Alan jumped onto a grass verge, rolled over and sprang to his feet.

'Richie! Come on! For fuck's sake jump.'

I jumped!

Absolute blackness. Time stopped. I saw myself in a bed. My parents on one side of it and a priest on the other giving me the last rites. Then a kind of voice was saying, 'You do realise that you are dying, don't you?'

'But I'm only a kid!' I complained.

'Yes I know.'

'I don't want to die. I'm too young to die.'

'I know exactly how old you are.'

'I don't want to die!'

'But you've thought about it quite a lot.'

'That's different.'

'Different?'

'Yes, different. I mean, I was just thinking about it.'

'Different or not you are dying and will soon be dead!'

'I'll make a deal with you.'

'A deal?'

'Yes.'

'Go on.'

'Give me my life back and I promise to try to do something good with it.'

'Something good?'

'Yes, just give me back my life please.'

'It's a deal!'

The blackness was filled with light and I felt as though I'd just been born again. It was weird beyond belief. I was now in bed looking up. I could see my parents' faces. They both looked terribly upset. I tried to speak but I couldn't. Their faces came closer and they spoke very gently to me. I couldn't make out what they were saying. I saw the priest and he was putting this oil and stuff on my forehead and was praying. My mother's voice broke through and I could hear her telling me that I'd had an accident and that I was a good boy and I'd be alright. It was like that time when she told me the same thing after I'd stolen the milk and my father had beaten me. I tried to speak. She put her fingers to my lips and the priest carried on giving me the last rites. I wanted to tell him to stop. There was no need, I'd made a deal. I wasn't going to die. I wanted to tell my parents this too but I couldn't speak. I knew that I was going to live and that I had to do something useful with my life in return. They thought I was going to die and I couldn't help their pain. It was crazy and weird and enchanted.

A couple of days, or was it months, later I'd recovered enough to speak and was told that as I jumped my foot had caught the moving wheel which dragged me down and under the wagon. My face was badly torn about and I nearly lost my right eye. I was packed in sandbags because I had so many broken bones. A priest came with two nuns and they gave me the last rites again. I let them do it but told them that there was no need. I was going to live. I'm sure they didn't believe me.

I don't know to this day if I had that conversation with some mystical being, God perhaps, or with my own inner imagination. I do know, however, that it was real and that, whatever it was, it saved my life. I've tried, through a whole series of failures, to keep my side of the bargain ever since. Some deal, eh?

Within no time at all I'd recovered enough to be taken back home by ambulance. But the journey from Oldham to Liverpool took its toll and within a couple of hours of arriving back home I was in the local children's hospital. The house was packed with relatives and well-wishers and a bed had been made up for me in the living room. I searched through the faces to find James. He was pushed to one side and told not to get in the way. I had to wait for all the fuss to die down, and only had a moment with him shortly before they took me off in another ambulance. His beautiful blue eyes said all there was to say. How lucky can a brother be? He explained later that he had not been allowed to come to the hospital to see me. Nor was he allowed to visit me in the children's hospital. There was only one thing for it. I'd have to get well real soon and go to see him. That's precisely what I did too. I got better and went home. That's when I heard about Rosemary, his girlfriend. He was so proud of her. I told him later that fourteen seemed a bit young to be going out with girls. He laughed and told me that she was special and I'd find out for myself soon enough. When I finally got to meet Rose I liked her instantly. She brought the best out in James and he was becoming all grown-up. He even started to call my father 'pop'. My father put up only token resistance and the new name had the effect of humanising him somewhat.

I missed a lot of school. Even when I was allowed back home I had to spend much more time in bed, which irritated me after a short time. I longed for the return to school. I was curious to find out from Alan what had happened to him after the accident and to see what kind of reception I'd get from him and the other kids. My mother kept me from going to school for quite some time. 'Doctor's orders!' she insisted. I would plead with her to allow me to go to school and she would explain that my bones needed time to heal properly. Once she said, 'It's a miracle that you're alive.'

I could only respond by saying, 'Yes. I know.' But I don't think she understood that I really did know it was kind of magical and enchanted the way I could survive things.

'You must have a very special guardian angel.'

'Yes, I guess so.'

Then my day arrived. I was to be allowed to visit the school. It was still by appointment and only to see the headmaster, but it was better than nothing. It was wonderful. I made my entrance quite deliberately at the wrong end of the school. This, you see, gave me the opportunity of passing down the central corridor and seeing into each classroom. Of course I could also be seen. At the end of the corridor I prepared for the most dramatic walk of my life. I'd left the walking stick at home. This way was far more dramatic. I saw myself being spotted by the kids in each classroom as I made the most of my limp. A senior boy in the corridor told me that the whole school had been praying for me twice a day. Fame at last, I thought. It was better than ever I could have hoped for. I had centre stage and I was going to make the most of it. Can you blame me? The headmaster, coming out of his office to see what all the fuss was about, saw me and greeted me with the kind of warmth usually reserved for old friends. He sent the prefect to fetch my form teacher. We had tea and biscuits together and I felt like a human being among equals. So warm was the welcome that I began to feel slightly, but only slightly, guilty for overdoing the limp. We talked about the accident and once again I was told that it was a miracle that I was alive. On the way out I had no choice but to maintain the same limp I'd arrived with. I felt deeply ashamed. I decided that by the time I was allowed to return to school full-time my limp would be gone. It very nearly was too. A miraculous recovery indeed.

When I finally did get back to school the headmaster had assigned a boy to look after me for a couple of weeks. As things turned out, this was the best thing that could have happened to me. His name was Laurie Clarke. He was an altar boy and he very quickly enrolled me there too. He did his job well, never allowing me to be pushed by the other kids or to carry anything. He'd meet me at the corner of the street each morning, walk me to church where we would serve at the altar for morning mass, walk me to school, carry my books, explain to the other boys all about my accident and how it was a miracle that I was alive. He was quite a charmer. He was there whenever I needed a hand. He even invited me to his youth club. It was a church-run club not far from home. I went mainly to repay him for his kindness. He introduced me to all his friends and told them all about the miracle. It was getting embarrassing. Then, halfway through the evening, when we were all sat on the steps outside the club I saw this boy. He was my age and was just getting off his bike. His healthy colour and thick black curly hair made him look like one of those Greek or Roman statues. He was greeted warmly by everyone. I was struck dumb. Laurie introduced us. His name was Mike.

Truth Denied

By the time I was fourteen the atmosphere at home had improved. Not least because in this new house there was space to avoid each other. It had seven bedrooms, a bathroom, three living rooms, a kitchen and a huge walk-in pantry. My father had landed a job as manager of a small building firm and his new wealth was reflected in the house which was furnished throughout. Quite a change from the old place. He was still drinking a lot and I failed to see how he could hide it at work. Somehow, though, he must have done. He was back to hiding the bottles behind his chair, which no one else was ever allowed to sit in. There was nothing new in him having his own chair. He'd always claimed the best one for himself.

The youth club where I'd met Mike was a place I came to feel at home in. Mike liked to play table tennis so I decided to learn and practised whenever I could. The idea being that when I was good enough I'd invite Mike to play. I practised and practised because I just wanted to be near him. I wanted his friendship more than anything in the world.

I was beginning to outgrow my clothes and became really quite particular about what I wore. I made demands about the kind of clothes my mother was buying and insisted that I was old enough to select the things I had to wear. If I'd have left things to her I'd still be wearing grey suits.

It was an exciting time. My inner world was merging more with my new outer world and my confidence was increasing. I was beginning to feel beautiful for the first time. I didn't have any spots like some of the kids my age and was longing for the day when I could start shaving.

The voice I'd heard that time when I had my accident was kind of with me and merged with me. It didn't talk to me or anything like that. It was just in a way there, deep within me. All rolled into me. It felt good.

School life too had improved dramatically, thanks solely to my new form master, Mr Kerrigan. He was a man who never once used the cane. Instead, he talked things through. I rose from being bottom of the class to second and when you consider there were over forty boys in the class you'll realise what an achievement that was. My search for answers drove me on in every subject. Because of my new interest in school I was made a prefect and was heralded as an example for other boys to follow. The feeling that I belonged to the priesthood was still around and found its outlet in being an altar boy. I still couldn't talk to anyone about it though. I knew, but I wasn't sure, if that makes any sense. For the first time in my life I felt integrated, whole.

Mr Kerrigan brought new ideas to the school. He would send us out on projects, which we'd write up and present to the class. He trusted us to go out on our own and do the work. I think it was the first time anyone had ever trusted me. I vowed never to break that trust.

I was on one of those projects that day. I'd been down to the docks to count ships, see where they came from and where they were bound. We had to find out what kind of cargo they carried, what kind of work dockers did and things like that. It was a marvellous project to be on. I warmed to the dockers instantly. Their sense of fun and their dirty jokes reminded me of school. I explained all about the project and they responded helpfully. These were the same kind of men who'd turned a blind eye to our gang's raiding parties years before. They'd known what we were up to and could have caught us if they'd really wanted. These were real genuine people. I sat with a group in a dockers' canteen called Stan Water's and heard all kinds of things. The dirty jokes I tried to remember for school. One man of about sixty asked me if I knew what the Dockers' Umbrella was. I blushed thinking it was going to be another dirty joke. He wasn't joking, though. He took me outside and pointed to the overhead railway.

'That, my son, is the Dockers' Umbrella.'

He anticipated my questions and went on to tell me that it was the first overhead railway in the world and had been given its name because the dockers would shelter under it in bad weather. He was a proud man, a man easy to like. He went on to tell me about how the men were herded like cattle into pens each morning. The chargehand would then select out those he wanted for the day's work. I was outraged that this should be the case but no more than this man himself. He spoke with sadness of how people were selected by their religions. That is, Catholics and Protestants. I had no idea which religion he was but I told him that I was ashamed to be an altar boy. He disapproved and told me that the future belonged to youngsters like me. I should never, he insisted, ever be ashamed of what I was.

'Just look to the future and change it for the better.'

I left him as he turned back into the dock gates. I felt a bit like a traitor because I had no intention of having anything to do with either the docks or Catholics and Protestants. I was tempted to run after him to explain that it was people like him who were the ones who should make the changes now. Stuff the future. I merely turned and watched him join a group of other dockers. I was left with the noises and voices of the canteen in my head as I made my way back home. 'Get some qualifications under your belt, lad, and stay away from the likes of this.'

My home was only a fifteen-minute walk from the docks and lost in thought I headed there.

'Excuse me, do you think you could help me?'

The polite question had come from a man of about thirty or so. A working man not unlike the men I'd just left.

'Yes, if I can. How?'

'Well, I'm locked out you see. Left me keys on the

kitchen table. Can't get in. There's a small window which goes into the kitchen which I can't get through. Would you mind climbing through for me and opening the kitchen door?'

'Sure. Where do you live?'

'Just through here. The next street.'

He pointed and began to lead the way. I followed prepared to do my good deed for the day. However, as we entered the back entry there was something about him which wasn't quite right. I couldn't put my finger on it but thought that perhaps he was using me to break into a house.

'You want me to climb through a window?' I said with suspicion in my voice.

'Yes, if you wouldn't mind. There's a table just under it in the kitchen. You'll see my keys on it. I'll give you some money...'

His explanation was convincing and I felt awful for having doubted him. I told him that it was alright and I didn't want any money. I followed him down the long back entry. He was walking very slowly and kept glancing at me. Perhaps he wanted me to break in to a house after all. I started to ask him questions about which house it was, what colour it was painted. Things like that. He stopped and took a cigarette packet from his coat pocket and leaned against the wall facing me.

'Smoke?'

'No thanks. Which house is...'

'You know what I want, don't you?'

'Yes, to climb through a window but I don't think that it's...'

He started to rub the front of his trousers and said, 'Not really.'

'Then why...'

'Come on, you know.'

I was beginning to get the idea.

'I'll pay you.'

It was now obvious that he had an erection and I became

both scared and intrigued at one and the same time. A voice in my head was telling me to get the hell out of there and another was saying stay.

'You know what it's like don't you. You do it don't you?'

As he spoke he reached out and touched the front of my trousers. I was rooted to the spot. I'd like to tell you it was with fear but I was getting a hard-on and he kept talking about wanking and things like that. Why did I let him do that? He undid the front of his trousers and showed me his erection. He began to masturbate.

'You do this don't you?'

How did he know? How could he tell? His hand went to my zip and as he began to pull it down he told me to get hold of his. I felt my hand rising towards it. He knew I did things like this, but how? Perhaps there was something about my face. I was just about to touch it when Mike came to my mind. Instantly, I took to my heels and ran for all I was worth. I was an altar boy not a wanker. Sure I'd done it with Pip in school but he was at least the same age as me and besides I knew him. Freaks like this man should be stopped, right? I mean, he could go on doing this to loads of lads for ages, right? At the corner of the street I went into a phone box and called the police. They told me to wait there and they'd send someone. I waited for half an hour before this policeman slowly arrived, on foot.

'Was it you who phoned?'

'Yes, but it's too bloody late now. He's well gone. I phoned ages ago.'

He waffled on about the police having lots to do and there being no cars available. I didn't believe a word he said. He took my name and address and asked me what had happened. I told him in graphic detail but left out the bit about getting a hard-on myself.

'You won't get him will you?'

'Perhaps no, perhaps yes. You've given a good description. Can't guarantee these things but you never know.'

His eyes told me that they wouldn't even look for the

man.

'Just forget it!' I said with anger and walked off.

I went to my grandmother's and had a cup of tea with her while she told me yet again about how important it was to go to mass and confession. I told her that it was all a waste of time considering the way things were on the docks.

By the time I got home there was a plainclothes policeman waiting to see me. You could have cut the atmosphere with a knife. My parents were with him and they were all drinking tea out of the best cups. The policeman asked me to tell him exactly what happened. I felt very embarrassed to do this in front of my parents but he insisted and so I told him. I felt like I was making something out of nothing and getting my family into trouble with the police. The policeman had been glancing at my parents while I'd been speaking and they were saying things to each other with their eyes which I didn't understand. When I'd gone over the story a couple of times the policeman asked me to wait in the next room while he had a word with my parents. I went through to the kitchen and made an enormous sandwich. I had plenty of time to eat it before I heard my father calling me. His voice came from the hallway and it said just one word.

'Richard!'

The atmosphere had perceptively changed. They seemed more relaxed and the policeman smiled and told me to have a seat. Then he began.

'Lads talk about these things, don't they? At school?'

How did he know?

'No,' I lied.

It was too embarrassing for words.

'We think they do,' he said disregarding my denial and nodding his head towards my father.

'Your dad tells me that you used to run away a lot.'

How could he? Keep things in the family, he'd said. Now he was telling them about me running away. Jesus! Did they know about the old man in the pictures and how I'd liked the way he touched my leg? I began to panic.

'That was ages ago.'

'You strike me as being old enough to understand these things,' he went on.

Jesus. He did know. I must have some sign over my head which people can see. It says 'Wanker' and has a flashing neon light with an arrow pointing to my head.

'You know what I'm driving at, don't you lad?'

'I think so,' I confessed.

'Right,' he said with relief. 'Strong imagination lads of your age, right?'

Then it hit me. He thought I was making the whole thing up.

'You don't believe me do you?' I said from one to the other.

'We've wasted enough of this man's time,' my father interjected.

'You don't believe me!'

'Look, we understand,' the policeman said.

I was horrified at their mutual alliance. Did they really think I'd make such a thing up? Yes they did!

'Richard! We are wasting time,' my father said firmly.

'Dead bloody right we are,' I said with anger.

'This has gone far enough. We know what boys are like...'

As my father spoke so they all began to stand up.

'We'll say no more about it,' he went on.

The next minute they're all shaking hands and my father was telling the policeman how sorry he was for wasting his time. I flew out of the room and headed for my bedroom. I slammed the door shut and then locked it. I'd show them. They were all the same, adults. One giant alliance. Bastards. I felt dirty again. If they could believe that I could make up such a thing then what did they actually know about me? Perhaps more than I realised. If that's the way things are, fine. That's okay with me. I masturbated. No, I wanked!

Pip was delighted at my return to our old routine and we began to meet almost every day. Never again would I tell the truth about sex to anyone. We met in school and out. He introduced me to a picture house were men gave you money to let them toss you off. He told me of a toilet where we could do the same thing. I abandoned myself to the new sport with relish. Vengeful relish. I'd make them pay. I got Pip to tell me everything he knew about the sport and of every place he knew. I tried each one and found places by myself. I masturbated a lot on my own too. It became that it was the only thing I could trust or rely upon. I stopped going to church and began to steal small things from shops and from school. Things I didn't want and would, more often than not, throw away afterwards. It was weird and I thought that perhaps I was going out of my mind. If I was bad then I was, at least, getting good at something!

The scene of the guy in the back entry with his cock in his hand telling me that I did the same thing replayed itself over and over in my mind. He'd been right. I did know about wanking and stuff. All that crap about being an altar boy and a priest was a waste of time. I was bad, real bad and I knew it too. I mean, I felt bad so I must be, right? I must give myself to it without reserve. I concluded too that I must be queer because I enjoyed it so much. There was no way out now apart from death. Why not? I mean, why not die? It had to be better than this. I was cracking up and going to pieces and no one apart from me knew it. I mean, why tell anyone? Who cares?

Easy Money?

Soon after that explosive abandonment of family and self I started to use the toilet and adjacent gardens at the top of the steet to pick men up. It was a kind of dare to do what I was doing in full view of the street where I lived.

At any time my parents could have seen me. I guess I hoped they would.

The toilet was set back in a garden just off the main road. I'd used it many times before but not as I was going to use it now. The first time I entered with new intentions my heart was racing and I had to admit to myself that I was scared. Of what? I'm not altogether sure. Perhaps, of not being found out. Inside my head though was an anger which demanded release. An anger which said, well, if they don't believe it, then go ahead and do it and make them pay for it. It was a crazy kind of disintegrated rejection which drove me. I was coming apart and in a strange kind of way what I was doing would keep me together. The momemt I entered a man left. A couple of men were standing around by the three cubicles, which were all being used. I used the stalls and left. I still wasn't sure quite how to do things. That is, how to read the situation. I mean, how do you know which man is interested and which is just using the bog? When I left a man followed and I thought he was going to follow me into the gardens. He didn't. He went straight to a car and drove off. I decided to sit on a bench in full view of the toilets, and our street, and count the men going in and out. That way, I figured, I would know when a cubicle became empty and I could go back in. So that's what I did. I sat and counted. Two in. One out. That meant five in there all together. That's when the man joined me on the bench.

'Lovely day.'

I was obliged to answer.

'Yes it's okay.'

'Been here long?'

I was losing count and inwardly cursed this polite man's conversation.

'Yes. A lovely day. It's picking up again.'

I lost count. Damn it. Why didn't he just piss off and leave me alone. I'd have to go back into the bog to see how many were in there now. I turned and looked at the man telling me how much the weather had improved since last week. He was about thirty years old, dressed like an office worker and spoke kind of posh.

'I hope I'm not disturbing you?'

I shook my head and told him it was okay.

'You seemed lost in thought.'

'No. It's okay. I was just thinking...' I didn't finish.

'I was on my way home and thought a breath of fresh air would do me good. Do you come here often?'

'Yes. I live just over the road.'

'A local boy?'

'Yes. Just over there.'

'Would you care for a cigarette?'

I took it and he lit it from an expensive-looking lighter. Within seconds I was coughing.

'I am sorry. Do forgive me. I should have warned you. They are French. Rather strong?'

'It's great,' I coughed.

'Please, you must allow me to buy you a soft drink.'

'No need. It's okay.'

'I insist. I should have warned you. Besides, a cool drink will ease your throat. I insist.'

'If you want...'

'Then it's settled,' he said, standing.

I stood too and headed for the shop across the road. It was at this point that I somehow knew he was picking me up. This he confirmed at the pavement.

'Look, why not come home with me. I have just the thing. It's not far and my car is just around the corner.'

I tried to figure out how to raise the subject of money but he was way ahead of me.

'I have some interesting photographs you might care to see and I'll make certain you have enough to get home with.'

'Okay.'

He relaxed instantly. His car was as smooth as he was. We drove for about twenty minutes and he talked about all kinds of things. I listened. His house matched the car. The poshest I'd ever set foot in. He brought cold soft drinks and we sat on a huge sofa in front of a gas fire which looked like a coal fire. When the drinks were finished he took the glasses back to the kitchen and on his return closed the curtains and put a small side light on. From somewhere behind a bookshelf he collected a shoe box. The kind of thing new shoes come in. He placed it upon my knee and said, 'The photographs!'

I took the lid off and there was a pile of photographs of stark naked boys. All about my age or younger. Photographs which had obviously been taken in this very room. As I looked through them he began to remove my clothes.

Afterwards, the excitement gone and guilt flooding in, I raced to get my clothes back on. He pleaded with me not to go and asked me to stay to take a shower.

'Let me at least give you your bus fare.'

He handed me an envelope which a quick glance told me contained more money than I'd ever seen.

'Same time next week.'

'Okay,' I agreed.

He insisted on driving me back to the gardens so I let him. I met him each week after that at the same time and looked through the shoe box and got my envelope. Easy money, right?

That bench in the gardens became my office and I was becoming a confident operator. Thoughts about being dirty and committing mortal sins came to my mind frequently but I was getting better at keeping them from surfacing. In no time at all I could spot a potential punter or other boys working the same toilets and gardens. A kind of agreement developed with the other boys that we wouldn't try to steal each other's punters. The agreement worked out well for us and kept the prices high. I once made the mistake of having sex with one of the other boys. It wasn't quite a disaster but we both waited for the other to do for each other what punters did for us. That is to suck us off. That's what 99 per cent of the punters wanted. I was making enough to buy new clothes and never once did my parents ask me where they'd come from. This angered me but it was also a relief. There were times I wanted them to ask me so that I could tell them the truth.

I stopped working that toilet and gardens after it was confirmed that I'd become the lowest of the low. Scum! I was in a cubicle when the familiar note appeared. I now carried my own pen to answer these notes. A price was agreed but this guy wanted to do it there in the cubicle. I upped the price and he agreed. What the hell, I'd done it before and had never been caught. He pushed the money through and told me to take my clothes off. It was as risky as anything but I did as he asked. That's when the door was pushed open and he came in with another man. I couldn't scream or shout or anything but I did my best to get them out. I told them to fuck off and take the money. They told me to shut up and thumped me one. I became terrified and struggled in the small space to grab my clothes. They tore them from my hands and began to hit me.

'You're not going anywhere until we've had our money's worth.'

I was trapped and figured that the sooner I could get them to come the sooner I'd be out of there. That was a serious mistake. I should have screamed my head off. Both of them forcefully entered me! I'd never had this done before. They left me bleeding and crying. I just cracked up and lay on the filthy floor feeling just as filthy. The bleeding scared me more than anything else but I knew I couldn't go to hospital. What could I tell them? I was doing punters in a public toilet and they raped me? No chance! I cleaned myself up as much as I could with bog paper then folded my handkerchief so that it acted as a pad and placed it inside my underpants. I felt sick and dirty, but it was my own fault. I'd brought it upon myself. I mean, let's face it, I was in the wrong.

The bleeding and the pain continued for days and days and I went through all the handkerchiefs I had. I swallowed a load of asprins in an effort to both ease the pain and put a stop to it altogether. This only made me sick and I vomited them back up along with everything else in my stomach. I vowed never to go back to those toilets. I couldn't set foot outside of the house for weeks. I avoided all conversation with my mother, and my father was hiding in his bottles of booze so he was no problem. Thoughts of suicide filled my head. It was a crazy couple of weeks. My mother did her best to find out what was wrong, much to her credit, but it was too late. How on earth could I tell her what had happened? It was very strange too because I was forever playing with myself. I mean, after what had happened you'd think that's the last thing I'd do. It was a further confirmation that I was scum, right? I thought about burning the toilets down but instinctively knew that it was the wrong place to burn down. I'd have to burn the whole damn city of Liverpool down with me in the middle.

The only escape I found throughout this pain was in my inner world of fantasy. I escaped in there as often as I could. I lived in there and became beyond touch. I could make believe it hadn't happened and that I was basically good. In my mind I became an altar boy again and went to mass every day.

Cracking Up

Avoiding my friends became increasingly more important to me. They thought I was a good and decent kind of boy. They knew I'd been an altar boy and had not the slightest idea what I'd become. I found their natural good natures too much to cope with. It kind of made me feel worse to be around them. I would see Mike in the youth club and feel totally unworthy of his friendship, yet I wanted it so much. I would see him and feel dirty. Nothing was good any more and I should've known that it wouldn't last. The times I did drop in to the youth club, just to see Mike, I experienced a distancing sensation. It was weird because Mike would always make a point of coming to meet me the moment I entered. I felt like a complete fraud and would drift out again, telling him I had things to do. I just didn't feel good enough. His looking out for me was like having salt rubbed in the wounds, if you know what I mean. The things I had to do amounted to going back home and sitting buried in the television set or books, never speaking to anyone. I knew I was kind of cracking up and welcomed it in a strange sort of self-punishing way. My only comfort continued to be masturbation but I always felt guilty about it afterwards.

After some considerable time of this self-enforced isolation my mother insisted that I go with her to see a counsellor. This took me by warm surprise and brought me that little bit closer to her. She was obviously seeing my pain. The counsellor was a woman of about my mother's age and seemed nice enough, but in front of my mother I just couldn't open up. To have asked my mother to leave would be like pushing her away and I wanted her close. I couldn't win so I said nothing. In the end the counsellor decided it might be a good idea to see us separately. She spent time with my mother first and then with me. I didn't understand anything she said; she was saying things in a way which I couldn't for the life of me make sense of. She was nice but that was it. At the end of my time with her she told me she was prepared to see me once a week and that if I liked I could join one of her weekly groups. I knew that she had something positive to offer even though I didn't know what and I agreed to join the group. What decided me was her genuine concern for me. What helped me was that she was a woman. It wasn't what she said that convinced me that I needed help, it was more the things she said with her body and her eyes while she spoke which told me I could trust her. I found that I didn't want to leave and this reminded me of the Chinese laundry when I'd sat and told the old Chinaman everything.

On the way home I told my mother that I was looking forward to the Saturday morning group. She was clearly pleased. When we arrived home, however, my father gave my mother the third degree and told us both that no child of his was going to see a bloody psychiatrist. My mother told him that it wasn't a psychiatrist and that the woman was a child psychotherapist.

'It's the same bloody thing woman. What's the matter with you?'

I exploded in defence of my mother and my lost opportunity.

'It's you who should see a psychiatrist!'

His punch sent me flying through the air and I landed on the far side of the room. As I picked myself up, with my mother's help, I realised that what I'd said must somehow be the truth. He reminded me of a jealous schoolboy. A couple of days later a letter of confirmation arrived from the adolescent unit and my mother tried to reason with my father. His response was to throw the letter onto the back of the fire.

'That's an end to it. I don't want to hear another word about it.'

I looked at the flames and saw myself going up in smoke. That evening I went out and ended up in the picture house where men paid boys to have sex with them. I let a man do anything and everything he wanted in the back row and didn't ask him for money. It felt real good.

Not long after that James joined the merchant navy. He was delighted to get away and I felt pleased for him and sad for me. I knew I'd miss him. Just before he left he had the most wonderful verbal fight with my father which, as far as I was concerned, he won. He was still seeing the same girl, Rose. So, with my brother and my cousin now in the merchant navy I was left with my younger sister who was the apple of my father's eye. She could twist him around her little finger. It was really strange the way he talked to her. With her he was remarkably gentle and kind. I was as jealous as hell. When she'd first been born I was about seven years old and I was jealous then too. I recall asking my mother one day while she was breast-feeding Kathleen if she liked the new baby.

'Oh yes, look at her, she's beautiful.'

'Do you like me?'

'Don't be silly. Of course I do.'

'No, I mean, do you like boys?'

'Yes, what are you getting at?'

'You know, she's the first girl and we're boys, are you glad?'

'I always wanted a girl.'

'Always?'

'Yes, but we had one boy after another.'

'Did you want a girl when you had me?'

'Richard, when I had you I thanked God.'

'But you wanted a girl, really.'

'We hoped for a girl but we were thankful for what God sent.'

'If I'd been a girl, you know, what would you have called me?'

'You're not a girl.'

'I know, but you must have had a name ready, right?'

'Alicia! But you're not a girl and that's that.'

I hated the name, especially when I discovered that it was my father's mother's name. Nonetheless, I recall trying very hard to behave like a girl just to please him. It wasn't that I wanted to be a girl, it was more that I tried to be his mother in a weird kind of way. To some extent it worked too. For a short time his interest in me grew. It didn't last though because I couldn't keep it up. But anything was worth a try. You see, when you feel that you're not wanted just for yourself, you have to be someone else. It's then like you don't exist and you have to do things to make your existence real. Even getting belted was a kind of confirmation that I existed. It was better than nothing. A cuddle or a slap, what's the difference?

Anyway, James had left home and gone to sea. How I envied his new found freedom. I'd lost my companion in the struggle to survive and needed a new one urgently.

Special Friends

The youth club was packed when I entered and they all wanted to know where I'd been hiding myself. If they only knew about the toilets and things then they wouldn't be so interested. I told them some story about what had kept me away and they accepted it, which only seemed to confirm to me that I was a fraud. Mike was nowhere to be seen. I asked about him as casually as I could and heard that he was getting ready for some exams at school and hadn't been in for a while. Not being able to ask much more I went into the coffee bar to see what I could learn from Jimmy Lynn, the man who organised the club. He could tell I was pumping him for information and said he hadn't realised that Mike and I were friends. I tried to brush it off as being not the slightest bit important.

'He's just a mate. So, what's new?'

Jimmy filled me in on what had been going on since I'd last been in and showed me some photographs of a trip the club had been on. I scanned the photographs for one of Mike and there he was. I asked Jimmy to tell me about it. Mike was beaming a smile straight into the camera and was wearing the same blue sweater he'd had on the first time I'd seen him arriving on his bike. Jimmy talked about the trip and then about friendship. He told me how important it was to have a special friend.

'The last time Mike was in he asked about you but I

could only tell him that you'd not been in.'

I nearly fell off the bar stool.

'Yea?' was all I could muster.

I wanted to know exactly what he'd said, how he was, what he was wearing, when was he coming in next, everything, anything.

'He's here next Tuesday evening. Playing in the table tennis match.'

That's all I needed to know. I wanted to throw my arms around Jimmy and thank him, but all I could come up with as I pushed myself back onto two legs of the bar stool was, 'Fancy a coke?' Before Jimmy could answer I fell head over heels off the slipping stool and everyone, including me, laughed themselves silly.

Tuesday was light years away. I wished I'd had the sense to take the photograph of Mike. Time dragged and everything I did seemed either to go wrong, or I'd break something, or I'd not hear what people were saying. My mother commented how she was glad that I was taking an interest in things. What things? I washed and ironed the shirt I would wear for the Tuesday. I had my favourite sweater cleaned. I even bought new underwear and socks and pressed the sharpest crease into my trousers. I had my hair cut and styled. I bought my first ever bottle of after-shave despite the fact that shaving was three years off. I cleaned my bedroom from top to bottom and did it again to make sure it was clean. I now had my own room with a single bed and it looked good. I polished my shoes and everyone else's and tidied up the sitting room. In all of this it never crossed my mind that I was creating such a fuss. My mother was delighted at my new found energy.

Then it was Tuesday and I was in pieces. I wasn't able to eat all day and I couldn't get myself together at all. It was well after eight when I finally left the house. At the corner of the street I remembered that I'd left my money on my bed and had to run home and get it. At eight thirty I entered the club and heard the match in progress. When I entered the match room there he was just changing ends. His eyes met mine and he smiled broadly. I gave him an encouraging wink which turned into a blushing smile. This in turn made me blush even more but I don't think he noticed. I prayed he hadn't anyway. I applauded every point he scored but in the end he lost and shook hands with the guy who beat him. He picked up his sweater and things and came directly over to where I was standing. Why in the name of God were my legs feeling like jelly? He put his arm on my shoulder and said,

'Hi!'

It was electric.

'Hi.'

Our eyes met and he told me that he'd played real bad and could have won.

'Next time, you'll kill him.'

'Right. Where have you been keeping yourself?'

'Bit like you, I guess, other things to do.'

'Exams eh?'

'Yes, kind of. Fancy a coke?'

'Thought you'd never ask,' he joked.

I was relieved to get off the subject of where I'd been keeping myself. He half held and half pushed me towards the coffee bar. We sat together and tried to catch up on what had been going on in the club. He told me that Jimmy had told him that I'd be in tonight. I felt myself blush.

'I'm glad you came, he said smiling.

'So am I.'

We then talked passionately about table tennis for quite a long time and he became very animated. At times, while he spoke, I would let my eyes wander over his face. He was singularly beautiful, smooth olive skin and dark shining eyes. I felt his eyes on me when I spoke and wondered what he thought of me. At times his searching eyes made me feel distinctly uncomfortable and I feared he might see too far in and see the bad bits. So powerful was this feeling that I'd shift uncomfortably and change the subject so that he'd have to talk instead. When other kids came round and tried to join in the conversation we excluded them and they got the message and left us alone. Then, as suddenly as it had begun, the evening was over. It was ten o'clock and the club was closing.

On the doorstep Jimmy told us about a meeting he wanted to hold to discuss the arrangements which would have to be made when the club closed for alterations. Six weeks closure was indicated. My heart sank. Six weeks without Mike! There was an added problem of where to hold the meeting because the club was booked up all the following week.

'You can hold it in our house,' I ventured.

'Are you sure that'll be alright?'

'Yes, I think so. I'll let you know. I'll phone you.'

'Terrific. But there's no need to phone. The club is open tomorrow night. I'll see you then.'

With all agreed I hung around for a while and talked some more with Mike and then reluctantly made my way home.

'See you tomorrow,' he called as he got up steam on his bike.

'Yes, see you,' I yelled back.

When I got home I went straight to my mother and asked her if we could have the meeting in the sitting room.

'When?'

'I'm not sure, soon though.'

'How many?'

'Not many.'

'How many?'

'I'm not sure.'

'Find out.'

'You don't mind though?'

'Find out how many first.'

I went straight to the telephone in the hallway and telephoned Jimmy at his home. He gave me all the information I needed. I hung on and called my mother, she called my father and it was okay'd. I don't think I'd ever been happier. I agreed to clean the sitting room on the night and set a fire in the grate. My mother suggested that she make some sandwiches and things and bring them in during our meeting. This would be the first time I'd brought friends home. In bed that night I panicked as I realised I'd not asked Mike for his telephone number. I replayed the whole evening over and over. I could recall every word, every gesture.

The following night in the club, as he put up a notice advertising the meeting, Jimmy thanked me and told me to thank my parents. Mike was the first to put his name on the list. I was second. As we looked at the notice together Mike said to me that our names looked good together. I agreed and gave him a playful thump on the arm. He returned it and dashed off saying, 'Come on, let's have a game of table tennis.' During the game I asked him if he was on the telephone at home and he told me that he was. We exchanged numbers.

The following day he phoned. I was delighted as I'd been too scared to call him. We chatted about this and that, then about the meeting. He said it might be a bit of a problem for him because it was likely to go on till late and he had to be home by half past ten.

'You could stay over.'

There was a silence which I thought would never end.

'That would be great. Are you sure it's okay?'

'Yes, hang on, I'll ask.'

'Okay, look, I'll ask my folks too.'

I checked with my mother and she readily agreed. The only question she asked about Mike was, 'Is he a Catholic?'

'Mother, it's a Catholic youth club.'

'Then that's okay then.'

'Mike? Yes, it's fine.'

'Yes, same here. Eh, that's great.'

When I put the phone down I dashed into the kitchen, threw my arms around my mother and told her that I thought she was the best mother in the whole damn world. I kissed her and she laughed and kissed me back.

'You're not so bad yourself.'

We infected each other with joy as we both set to prepare for the meeting and Mike staying over. Despite the seven bedrooms my mother suggested that Mike share my room. There was no objection from me. We shared the cleaning but my mother clearly made every effort and did far more than she needed to. I thanked her for making such an effort and told her that I loved her very much.

'Well, you've got friends staying, it's only right that I make them welcome.'

The day of the meeting came and not only had she put a vase of flowers in the sitting room but also one in my bedroom. I had to force back the tears when I saw it. It was such a beautiful thing to have done, don't you think?

Mike's father dropped him off and he was the first to arrive. I showed him my room and he said it was smashing.

'You can share with me or you can have my brother's room. He's in the navy.'

He threw his bag on the bed and simply said, 'This is fine.'

The meeting was a great success and my mother was a hit with everyone. She'd made a great effort and supplied us with a first-class spread. Mike thought she was fantastic and I was thrilled. He helped clear up afterwards and told me that our house was like a first-class hotel. This caused me to relook at it. It was kind of well done and I felt a twinge of guilt for not having really noticed before. Somehow, up until the moment Mike had said that, I'd carried a picture of the house inside my head which more accurately fitted the old house. I really hadn't taken in the changes. It was weird. I looked around and saw a huge, beautifully furnished house. My mother liked Mike a lot, especially when she discovered he had Irish blood.

I closed the bedroom door behind us and put the bedside light on. I'd always disliked central ceiling lights. Our voice tones changed to match the soft lighting and we began to undress. We matched each other item for item. With shirts off I was struck by his olive-skinned torso. Like my own it was smooth but his was as olive-coloured as his face. I usually slept raw these days but decided to keep my underpants on. That's when he told me that he thought I had a great body. I told him that so did he and we both laughed. With that he leapt into bed and asked, 'Which side's mine?'

'Take your pick.'

He opted for the side furthest from the door and dived under the covers. I put the light out and got in. We cuddled in to each other and said not a word. I felt at home with him. Words were not needed. However, just before I fell asleep I whispered to him, 'Mike?'

'Yes?'

'I really like you.'

He moved closer so that our noses were almost touching and through the moonlight I could see his eyes.

'I like you too Rich. I've never had a friend like you.'

I was starting to get erect and he was too.

'I think we should turn over and get some sleep,' I suggested laughing.

'I think you're right,' he said.

We turned over and slept with as much of our backs touching as possible. When I woke the following morning he'd turned over and was cuddled right into me. I stayed there, awake and at home with my new friend.

In the bathroom we laughed and touched a lot. He told me that he wished he was as broad as me and I told him that I wished I had his olive skin. By the time this mutual admiration society got down for breakfast, the others had eaten and my mother had laid the table for the two of us. She closed the dining-room door after serving and left us to each other. We talked and talked and talked. I questioned him about his favourite colour, the people he liked, the kind of school he went to, what his brother was like, how long he'd had his bike – in fact everything I could think of. His questions were much as mine and we would have been sat there still had my mother not insisted that she clear up.

We became firm friends. We stayed in each other's homes on alternate weekends and when we didn't see each other in the club we'd telephone. We each arranged our lives around the other. Invitations from other kids at the club to go to parties always included our two names. I felt complete. He was more than I could have hoped for. More, indeed, than I had hoped for. The only time I felt in danger of losing him was when he spoke about girls. They never entered my mind and I was becoming to accept that perhaps I really was homosexual. We would sometimes double date a couple of girls but we never had sex with them or anything and when we slept together we always reafirmed our bond. This bond we called friendship and that's precisely what it was. But more than that, for me it had become love and here he was taking more and more of an interest in girls. It was natural for him, I guess. Just as natural though was that sex between us was always a possibility but which I non-verbally opted not to actualise. It was best that way, I figured. I mean, sex was part of the bad side of me and my love and friendship with Mike was beautifully pure. Time and closeness with him was enough.

We'd arranged to meet in town to do some shopping on the Saturday morning and then he was to spend the weekend at my home. I met his bus and off we went. His love of music took us to Frank Hessey's music store. Mike just wanted to look and price a few items which was fine by me. All the music I needed I carried in my head. Mike became completely absorbed in the shop and that's when I saw the man take the trumpet from the stand and slip it under his coat, in broad daylight and in a crowded shop. I sent an elbow into Mike's ribs and told what I'd seen. The man saw us looking and made for the door. I met Mike's eyes which had become quite excited and we legged after the man in unison. As we gained on the man he dropped the trumpet and carried on running. The thief in me told Mike to let him go and we stopped and picked up the stolen trumpet. When Mike handed it back to the shop assistant I could see that he didn't believe Mike and I was furious. The same old shit. Tell the truth and no one believes you. Later, in a coffee shop, I told Mike about the man in the entry and how no one believed me, not even my own parents. He comforted me and I regretted telling him for I'd brought two worlds together that had no part in each other. We concluded that adults really didn't have much idea what it was like to be young and took a bus back to my home.

Getting off the bus at Bedford Road we window-shopped our way along the road. It was the men's clothing stores which held our attention more than any others and we pointed out the things we liked. He really was quite conservative the things he picked. But that was okay because he was Mike. That's when the car horn sounded, and turning around my heart sank and my legs became like jelly. I recognised both the car and the driver only too well. It was Shoebox. You know, the posh man with the shoebox full of nude photographs. He was waving. Shit! I turned away. The horn sounded again. He was calling me over. Oh dear sweet Jesus make him go away, I prayed. Mike was curious. He mustn't know about this. He mustn't know.

'Hang on a minute Mike. I'll be right back,' I said leaving Mike standing as I crossed the road towards Shoebox.

Shoebox must have thought that I was pleased to see him the way I ran to him.

'Hi,' I said, out of breath.

'My, how you've grown. For a moment I didn't recognise you.'

I wished that he hadn't.

'Your boyfriend?' he nodded towards Mike who was looking over.

'No way! He's just a mate.' I tried to sound as casual as I could.

'Does he...play?'

'No he doesn't!' I said coldly.

'Pity. Beautiful boy.'

'No way!'

'Pity. How are you anyway?'

'I'm okay. Got to go though.'

'When am I going to see you again?'

'Tomorrow,' I lied.

Holy shit! Mike was crossing the road towards the car.

'What time?'

'Half past two, here. Okay?' I said moving away.

'Yes, half past two. I've some new photographs to show you which I know you'll appreciate.'

Mike was now standing at my shoulder. Did he hear?

'Okay, see you then,' I said trying to walk away.

He spoke directly to Mike.

'Hello, I was just saying...'

Oh dear God, make him shut up!

'...what a lovely day it is. You must be...'

'Mike.'

Jesus Christ! They were shaking hands. The same hands that, well you know. My hurry to get away was obviously confusing Mike for he looked to me for some kind of explanation.

'At the same school?' Shoebox asked.

'No,' said Mike. 'The same youth club though.'

'We're going to be late, Mike. For tea! My mother's going out and...'

'The same club, which one would that be?'

Mike told him. He went on to tell him how good it was and of his love of table tennis. He told him what nights of the week it was on and everything. I had frozen to the spot. What next?

'Oh, I musn't keep you boys. You'll be late for tea. Richard, I'd hate to embarrass you at your club... You did say two thirty didn't you?'

I cursed him inwardly. He had me by the balls.

'Yes, that's right,' I said politely.

'I'll be waiting.' He whistled as he drove off.

Mike thought he was a really nice person and told me that I'd behaved rudely and could have been more polite. We nearly had our first fight. But lies saved the day. I explained to Mike that Shoebox was the man who organised the altar boys for our school and was a bit of a pain always making sure we turned up on time.

'Besides, my mind was on that thief and the trumpet and things, and the way the shop assistant didn't believe you, you know.'

Mike forgave me instantly and I felt like shit. Later, I told Mike that I had a real bad headache and would need to go to bed alone. Once again, he understood and once again I felt like shit. But, you see, I had to get rid of him for his own good. I mean, I had to show up for Shoebox the next day or else he'd wait outside the club or even worse, he'd go in. Mike went home and phoned me when he arrived to ask how I was. For Christ's sake!

I met Shoebox, we went through the usual ritual and I came away with my envelope. It was then that he told me he was a teacher.

I didn't go to the club during the following week because I knew Mike would ask me how I was and I'd be forced to lie again. On the Thursday I telephoned him and tried to explain that I'd been a bit under the weather.

'Rich, I called before and your mum said you were at your auntie's last Sunday.'

'Yes, for a while, that's all.'

He knew I wasn't being honest with him.

'Rich, are you alright. I mean, is anything wrong?'

'Nothing. No, nothing, why?'

'Nothing?'

'Mike, I'm alright. What is this?'

'Do you want me to come down?'

Oh God, the tears were falling all over the damn phone and I didn't know what the hell to say or do.

'Rich?'

I took a deep breath.

'Yes?'

'Shall I come down to yours?'

'Not tonight Mike.'

'Rich, I know something is wrong. I know you. So why don't you tell me? Come on.'

'Mike, please don't ask me...' I cried. 'Please don't ask me. Promise me you won't ask.'

'Eh, come on. Calm down. It's okay. I won't ask. Okay. Okay?'

'Thanks.'

'I'll see you next week then? But if you want, you can call me, yes?'

'Okay.'

When we hung up I stood by the phone unable to move. I was crying great heaving sobs. I couldn't tell him. I had to protect him from my truth. My mother must have heard the sobs for she rushed into the hall asking, 'What in the name of God is wrong? Is Mike alright?'

'He's fine. He's coming to stay next week.'

'Fine, but is he alright?'

'Of course he's alright.'

'Then in God's name what's wrong with you?'

She held me close in her arms for a minute or two then dried my tears with her apron.

'Are you in some kind of trouble?' she wanted to know.

'No. No trouble. You needn't worry. I'm okay.'

I pushed past her and went up to my room and fell fast asleep on my bed. I woke in the middle of the night, cold. I decided to have a hot bath.

After a long soak in the tub I returned to my bedroom draped in a bath towel. I caught sight of myself in the dressing-table mirror and went over to it. What I was looking for was unclear. Just me I guess really. What I saw was duality. There in the one image was both the loyal friend and the boy who had sex with men for money. I looked long and hard to see what it was that men could see in me. I saw a scared kid. I looked, too, to see what it was that Mike saw in me and I saw a phoney.

I spoke out loud. That is, one part of me spoke to the other. Crazy, right?

'I like Mike.'

'You're a queer!'

'I just like him!'

'Fucking dirty queer!'

'I don't understand anything.'

'I go with men for money and I really like it.'

'It's just the sex I like. I don't like them.'

'I'd love to have sex with Mike!'

'No I wouldn't. Not Mike!'

'I'm crazy!'

'No. Not really. Just fucked up in the head. It's not the same thing.'

'I'm queer. Can't deny that!'

'Yes, but with Mike it's beyond that. Beyond sex. Beyond everything.'

'Love? Piss off! That's just another word for queer!'

'It's love. It's pure.'

'Bullshit!'

'It's true. It's weird but it's true.'

'I know different, right! I know what I think about, right?'

'That's different.'

'I go with men for money!'

'I don't want to.'

'I do it!'

'I don't enjoy it.'

'My body does though!'

'It's not the same.'

'That's just crazy talk.'
'Mike is love not sex.'
'Sex is love.'
'It's not. Sex is men and money.'
'My body likes it.'
'I am my body.'
'I like it.'
'Sex pollutes love!'
'Keep them apart then.'
'Yes, yes, apart.'

I moved slowly away from the mirror and climbed into bed fearing for my sanity yet feeling that I should talk to myself much more in the future. Crazy as it was, it kind of helped me. I wished that there was someone I could go to to try and explain all the confusion. But there was no one, just a crazy image in a mirror.

Fighting Back

It was one of those nights when Mike was out with a girlfriend and I'd long since given up the idea of making up foursomes to be near him. My cousin was on leave and was going to the pub with my father. I was reading a book about some pop star and my fallen hero was taking the piss.

'You still into all that?'

When they arrived home from the pub they were both drunk and my father sent his supper crashing into the back of the fire with a curse. He raised his hand as though to hit my mother. What I did next came out of pure reaction. I jumped up from my chair and grabbed my father by his coat lapels. I lifted his sixteen stones off the ground and sat him down on the rug in front of the fire.

'If you ever, ever lay another finger on my mother or anyone else I swear to God I'll kill you!'

His face was white as a ghost with shock. I'd stunned the room into silence. My cousin stood silently as did my mother. I stormed out and headed up to my room. My fallen hero followed me, caught up with me halfway up the stairs and hit me one almighty blow under the chin. The remarkable thing was I didn't seem to feel it.

'Don't you ever hit your father,' he commanded.

'Look, I'll never forget you took his side or that you hit me. Now, piss off.'

I went into my room and he tried to follow so I grabbed my coat and went downstairs just to see if my mother was alright. She signalled that she was so I went out. Within the hour I'd earned enough from the local toilet to go downtown. I headed for Lime Street station where I'd heard from other boys and punters that business was brisk. Twenty minutes after getting there I was sitting in a restaurant with a punter. A pleasant enough man who entertained me lavishly and allowed me to tell him all about my family and Mike. I had sex with him later and refused his money. He'd given me what I'd needed so I gave him what he needed. It was fair enough and he told me about London. A place called Piccadilly Circus where boys charged a fortune. A place to remember.

As had now become the norm, I left the house with no clear notion of a destination in mind. I was without purpose. It was just important to get out into the potential life-giving air. Outside, I could breathe, I could feel the chains fall away. Usually the chains just melted from consciousness as my feet hit the steps leading from the house to the street. Today, though, my head was all fucked up and the chains stayed with me as I left the house. If I stayed at home I tended to end up being all wrapped up in the damn chains. Going out gave me another chance to find some purpose and identity. It was as though I went out kind of empty and allowed the experience of what came to fill me up. Whatever came, became me. Know what I mean? Each time I went out I hoped and prayed that I'd find myself. A self I could live with. Then I could bring it home and be it. More often than not, however, I brought home a depressed, fucked-up Catholic rent boy and I didn't care for that at all.

Today, my confidence was at an all-time low and the depressions had become top dog. I avoided eye contact with people and could only think about being a Catholic queer rent boy. Walking through the streets I seemed to see nothing but I felt everything. I walked and tried to make sense of my life, but I couldn't. Thoughts flew into my head and before I could do anything with them they were pushed out by new ones. I walked slowly but my mind was speeding and I felt as though it would crash and I'd go out of my mind altogether. I almost welcomed the notion of going crazy because that would be one way of explaining my fucked-up life to myself. Death was another alternative. Yes, to die would solve it all in one go. I didn't want to die, you understand, I just wanted the pain to stop. Death held the answer. That way I'd come face to face with the ultimate reality, God, and he would explain everything to me.

Today, my life had no colour to it. It was like a black and white film. Mostly black though. It was hopeless, sad and all fucked-up. I felt utterly alone. But there's always God, right? So I prayed, I begged him to help me. Nothing! There was never an answer when I prayed. I figured that I should have to pray in a church so I found one – there were plenty about. I stood in the back, letting my eyes wander down the aisles and along the walls. Though I'd never set foot in this church before, I knew it. It looked just like all the other Catholic churches in Liverpool. I stood there, at the back of the church, for ages, looking. I was looking for a sign. Hope. I prayed, 'If you're real, please help me.' Nothing! There never was. It's all a fake. A trick. Father Christmas wrapped up in rituals. Phoney. These thoughts scared me because if they were true that meant I really was on my own and I didn't think I could make it on my own. I'd asked God to help me in the street and there was no answer. I'd asked him in church and there was still no answer. What now? My grandmother always lit candles. An offering? That was it! I'd not made an offering. I lit a candle and said a prayer, 'For the love of God help me!' Nothing! It was all space and no touch. I gripped the bench in front of me and could feel the panic inside. I searched the church with my eyes. A light over a confessional box. A priest. There was a priest here. That had to be it. It was a sign, right? I almost ran to the box. There's always hope see? Never give up hope. I knelt in the box and became overwhelmed by guilt. The guilt of having sex with men, for money and for free. The boy in the mirror was there, right before my eyes, telling me that I'd enjoyed it and to stop being phoney about it. He recalled all the sex. All of it, in graphic detail. All the times men touched me in parks, toilets, cinemas, buses, fairgrounds, school. I couldn't shut him up. These things happened because I was me. Simple. It was me that caused these things to happen. The priest coughed. He was waiting for me to say something. I stood up and left the church.

The river Mersey looked incredibly inviting. It was full of touch. It would wrap itself around me and carry me with it wherever it went. It would never give me up. It would hold me to itself without judgement or question and become part of me. The river looked dirty and its waves were covered in oil. That was good. It was perfect, in fact. All that stood between me and it was the railing which was cold to the touch. I gripped the cold railing tightly and let the cold enter my hands. Nothing was forever. Not even the railings. When these railing had rusted away, others would take their place and the river would keep on flowing. The river would eventually cleanse itself of everything which men now polluted it with. The river had a future. I, on the other hand, had none. Death in the river was a better option. All I had to do was climb over the railings and join the everlasting river. The ultimate reality wasn't God. It was the river. Death.

'Looks cold doesn't it?'

I thought the question had come from inside my head so I answered it silently.

'Yes, kind of cold warmth.'

'Saw you standing here, see...'

The voice was alongside of me.

'...and I... It's busy today. Plenty of ships.'

I was startled by the intrusion and looked to my left to see him, a man. It's always a man. Like a fly, he'd found something rotten to feast upon. I stared at him, which caused him to speak again.

'That's a Blue Funnel Line isn't it?' He pointed to a ship in the centre of the river.

I continued to stare at him. He became all the men I'd ever known, had sex with, been touched by, loathed.

'Aren't you cold?' he asked.

Like all the others he wanted to sound friendly. I knew what he wanted.

'Why don't you just fuck off and leave me alone?'

'I'm sorry?'

'Just leave me alone can't you?'

I couldn't work out why I was sobbing.

'Are you alright?'

'Fuck off!' I screamed at the top of my voice.

He reached out to touch me.

'Keep your filthy fucking hands off me you dirty bastard.'

'Look, son, come away from here...'

'I'm not your fucking son!'

Other people began to gather and a man asked, 'You okay kid?'

For fuck's sake leave me alone, all of you...'

I ran, and ran, and ran.

Carried along like a leaf on the wind I went with it. Drivers of cars cursed at me to look where I was going and didn't seem to realise that they were supposed to run me over. Suddenly, I stopped and asked myself, Why? I was going out of my mind. I was closer to cracking up than I can tell you. I looked up and recognised the building in front of me. It was now dark but there were lights on inside. Eventually I pressed the bell. The door opened but I didn't recognise the woman who answered.

'Hello, what can we do for you?'

'Is this, erm, I mean is this, you know, is the woman in?'

'Mrs Johnstone?'

'I'm not sure...'

'The counsellor?'

'Yes.'

'I'm sorry love, they're well gone. They close at six. I'm just the cleaner...'

It was hopeless.

'...But I can ring her if you want, if it's important...'

'No, it's okay.'

'If it's important, she told me to ring her if it was important. Are you sure love?'

'No. It's not important. I'm sorry.'

As I walked away she called after me.

'Let me ring her, love... Can I tell her who called?'

'Okay.'

It wasn't until I was in the next street that I realised she was asking me my name. I turned back to tell her and the door was shut. I carried on walking.

I was tired of walking but couldn't take a bus or anything because I had no idea where I was going. I didn't know why I was going and I didn't care one way or the other. It crossed my mind that the man at the river was probably okay and I'd made a fool of myself. It was better not to trust men, though, if I didn't want to get hurt. But perhaps, if I did get hurt... I mean really hurt. You know, killed. That was almost better than the river, right? It had more justice to it. So far, I'd put myself in relatively safe situations with men and I didn't reckon I'd been hurt beyond what I'd deserved. What if I went with a real, rough, tough-looking man? I mean, kids do get killed, right?

I stood outside the main line railway station on Lime Street and waited for him. The man who'd do it. It wasn't long before men approached. First, a handsome young man of about twenty and then a whole stream of others. I put them all off by acting like I didn't know what they wanted. If that didn't work I asked them if they were queer or something. That sent them packing. I was there for hours before I saw him. He was rough, real tough-looking and when he spoke to me he was staggering and smelt of booze. He was perfect. He didn't waste time either.

'How's business?'

'Kind of slow.'

'How much?'

'That's up to you?'

'How long for?'

'As long as you want.'

He gave me a weird kind of look and questions darted across his face but I guess the booze told him the answers he wanted to hear. He called a taxi and we got in. He really stank of booze. He'd obviously gone drinking straight from work judging by his clothes. His conversation consisted of burps, farts and apologetic gestures as he bounced around in the cab. His face looked as though he was a boxer and so did his hands. He was an ugly son of a bitch. I could imagine the hovel he must live in.

But it wasn't! It was a perfectly clean and tastefully furnished semi. He threw his coat on the back of the chair, pointed to a cabinet and said, 'Help yourself to a drink. I need a piss. A whisky for me.'

When he came back into the room I was still trying to find the whisky and my heart was racing with anticipation and fear. I hoped he'd do it quick. He grabbed me, flung me around, and kissed me full on the lips.

'You're beautiful.'

He was loathsome.

'Upstairs.'

It sounded like an order and he pushed and pulled me towards the stairs and then up them. When we entered the bedroom he began to pull at my clothes. My shirt ripped and he mumbled an apology. I took it off along with everything else and waited for him to pounce. He pushed me back onto the bed and collapsed on top of me. This was it! Nothing! Then, snoring? Yes, he was bloody well snoring. My killer was asleep on top of me. I pushed him off and cracked up laughing, in an hysterical sort of way. I could have been crying, I'm not sure. Fuck it! Having thrown all caution to the winds I climbed under the sheets and cried – or was it laughed – myself to sleep.

I woke when he entered the room. He had obviously bathed and was wearing a bathrobe. In his hands was a tray.

'I've made you some breakfast.'

He was different. Soft. Like a big teddy bear. I sat up and looked around to get my bearings. He put the tray on my knees and said, 'I'll leave you to it.'

At the door he spoke, without looking at me. 'I've run a bath for you, when you're ready.'

Then he was gone. It was crazy, right? I mean there was my killer serving me breakfast in bed. I looked at it. It looked good, smelt good and tasted even better. On the tray was a tiny vase with one flower in it. I couldn't believe that such a rough tough man could do such a thing. I went to the bathroom, soaked in the hot water and put on the robe. My clothes had gone. What the hell was going on? I crept downstairs with the tray like a cat, ready to run. Music was coming from the kitchen, music which seemed out of place for it was opera. It was all so crazy. I looked into each room as I passed and saw beauty. Weird. I took a deep breath and walked into the kitchen. He was sat reading a newspaper and there were my clothes all clean and folded on an ironing board. The shirt had been perfectly repaired. I just stared at him then at the clothes.

'I'm sorry about last night... I was drunk... I know that's not a good enough excuse... You see... my mate... a workmate... a good man...well, he was badly injured in work... I'm a docker... I've done your gear.'

He was pointing to the clothes.

'Yes, I saw.'

'The shirt should be okay.'

'It's fine. No problem...'

I let my hands wander over my clothes on the ironing board.

'... Are you okay?' I asked.

'Yes. Are they okay?'

'Yes, great. Thanks.'

'Could you drink some tea?'

'If you're making some, yes.'

I couldn't make sense of any of it. When he stood to put the kettle on I instinctively rushed across to him and threw my arms around him. He held me tight. Real tight. He began to apologise for his behaviour all over again and I told him that it was as much my fault as his. I kissed him and made love with him there in the kitchen. It was the first time that I'd had sex and love all at the same time. It was beautiful.

We made no arrangements to see each other again. It was what it was. A once and for all happening which could never be repeated. He kept thanking me and I kept thanking him. Money was not mentioned and I left him about noon and took a bus home. I had been touched deeply and felt I owed him my life. I never saw that beautiful man again.

When I arrived home I was expecting all hell to break loose. You know – 'Where have you been? We've been worried sick.' They must have assumed that I'd stayed with Mike because they didn't ask. I wanted to tell them that I'd made love to a huge docker on his kitchen floor and that I was homosexual. They didn't ask so I'd have to let them know that I hadn't stayed at Mike's.

'Has Mike phoned?' I asked.

'No,' my mother replied.

'What? Not at all?'

'Not since yesterday. He said he had to go to his aunt's in Derby somewhere.'

Then she knew, they knew, that I'd not stayed with him. So why didn't they ask?

'I thought about killing myself yesterday,' I said to the space between them.

'Don't talk such nonsense,' my mother scolded.

The space between them seemed frozen in time and I heard it say, 'Don't kill yourself please, we love you so very much.'

'Bloody nonsense!' my father said.

'You don't give a damn anyway.' And hoped they'd say they did.

'Is Mike coming tonight?' my mother asked.

She used this kind of ploy to change the subject whenever things got too difficult to handle. I'd seen her do it many times.

'How the hell do I know. I've not seen him, have I?'

My father raised his head and I saw questions in his face but he closed his eyes and put his head back into his hand. He said nothing more.

Mike telephoned to tell me of their family trip to see his aunt in Derby. His father had made a real big deal of stopping at all the service stations. I didn't want to hear how good a father he was. I tried to tell Mike about how I'd been feeling the previous day but he kept on about his bloody perfect father. Then he told me about this real nice girl he'd met and how beautiful she was. I wanted to tell him that I'd made love to a man and wanted it to happen again and again. He went on about the girl.

Afterwards I lay on my bed and allowed thoughts to come and go. Thoughts of men and thoughts of girls. I was convinced that I was now a fully paid-up member of the homosexual world and I knew too, from priests and teachers, that homosexuality was not only a mortal sin but a mental illness as well. If that's the way thing were then so be it.

A couple of months later, when I'd just turned fifteen, I left school. By which time I'd come to recognise that my need to have sex for money with men was because in a way they loved me, cared for me, paid attention to me, wanted me. Like with that docker. These men supplied everything I'd ever wanted so I supplied what they wanted. What's wrong with that?

After one almighty verbal fight with my father I started to think about leaving home for good. London came to mind. What was the name of that place? Piccadilly Circus, right?

On The Game

Watch for punters
Learn the score
Money first
Then his pleasure
Make the punter
Want you more
Be the weakness
For his strength
Be the child
He's yet to have
Be the strength
For his weakness
Apologise
For saying, 'Dad.'

(Richie J. McMullen)

Also by Richie McMullen:

Enchanted Youth

It's 1958, and just turned fifteen, Richie leaves his Liverpool home bound for London, believing that boys can earn a fortune on the game. He discovers a world of rent boys preyed on by criminal gangs yet giving each other comfort and support; the excitement of Soho in the rock'n'roll years; and love for a public schoolboy his own age. When the boy's parents banish their son to Singapore to keep them apart, Richie joins the merchant navy and sets off in quest of his friend.

While his first volume of memoirs was, in his words, a journey through abuse to prostitution, *Enchanted Youth* leads him through a still more perilous time, from prostitution to love.

"McMullen emphasizes the good in people rather than the sordid or demeaning... in this sensitive, revealing memoir." -- *Publisher's Weekly*

"A deeply humanist protest against sexual exploitation... informs McMullen's work." -- *Gay Times*

ISBN 0 95449 134 1   £5.95pbk

Male Rape: Breaking the Silence on the Last Taboo

In a male-dominated culture, men do not want to accept their role as victims. In this groundbreaking work, Richie McMullen challenges the position of English Law that does nothing to recognise the existence of this under-reported but increasingly prevalent crime.

This critical study argues across the whole spectrum of abuse cases, identifying possible causes and re-evaluating the threat as a problem for us all to face, whatever our sex. It tackles basic issues of male sex aggression and liberation, concluding with research profiles and counselling advice for victims and those who help them; it courageously foregrounds a crisis few of us want to hear about.

"This is a fine, campaigning book with a wealth of detail and pungent observations... an important and authoritative work -- *Community Care*

"This book is an extremely powerful argument in favour of getting men to think carefully about what it actually means to be a *man* and to be *masculine*. McMullen has definitely broken new ground... we need more voices to accompany his." -- *Gay Community News*

ISBN 0 85449 126 0 £9.95 cased

Some other titles in our series of Memoirs by gay men:

Jack Robinson
Teardrops on My Drum

Liverpool in the 1920s: still Dickensian in its poverty, a city of docklands and back alleys, barefoot kids running wild in the filthy streets, bizarre eccentrics and sectarian violence. This is the world marvellously evoked by Jack Robinson in the story of his boyhood: forced to fend for himself from the earliest age, searching the city for adventure, love and sex, and joining the army as a 14-year-old boy soldier.

"A fascinating autobiography with its evocative descriptions of life in the Liverpool of the 1920s" – *Time Out*

ISBN 0 85449 003 5 £5.95 pbk

Jack Robinson
Jack and Jamie Go To War

This second volume starts in 1937, with the 15-year-old hero back in his home town after his spell as a boy soldier. The action ranges from Liverpool under the Blitz, through D-Day, via New York, South Africa and the Allied landings in Naples. It sees Jack as a wartime commando, then a seaman with the convoys, caught up in mutiny and racketeering, and always in pursuit of boys.

ISBN 0 85449 077 9 £5.95 pbk

GMP books can be ordered from any bookshop in the UK, and from specialised bookshops overseas. If you prefer to order by mail, please send full retail price plus £1.50 for postage and packing to:

GMP Publishers Ltd (GB),
P O Box 247, London N17 9QR.
For payment by Access/Eurocard/Mastercard/American Express/Visa, please give number and signature.
A comprehensive mail-order catalogue is also available.

In North America order from Alyson Publications Inc.,
40 Plympton St, Boston, MA 02118, USA.

In Australia order from Stilone Pty Ltd,
P O Box 155, Broadway, NSW 2007, Australia.

Name and Address in block letters please:

Name ______________________________

Address ______________________________

____

____